JONATHAN MEADES

POMPEY

Portsmouth: A nightmarish brick grid set on mud and populated by garish freaks, the setting for a novel unlike any you will read. Part hallucinatory adventure, part unhappy family saga, part perverse tragedy of fundamentalist delusion...

After using this book please wash your hands. Thank you.

'Disgusting and brilliant...a torrent of obsessive, angry imaginative fireworks...The prose...should earn Meades justifiable comparisons to such modernist novelists as James Joyce and Louis Ferdinand Celine, Thomas Pynchon and Martin Amis' *Paul Spike, Vogue*

'A vast, deranged epic... there is more invention in a single page of *Pompey* than many young British novelists manage in fifty.' *Richard Preston, Harpers & Queen*

'Dazzlingly... clever ... *Pompey* is the product of a brilliant mind.' *Nick Hornby, TLS*

'A *stupefacient* epic: its words have the power to astonish intoxicate... Its visionary grandeur is so blithely ambitious it defies you not to trawl through its hells of crushed viscera and velvet.' *Ian Penman, Time Out*

PUBLISHED BY JONATHAN CAPE

Photography David Thompson

box office **071 730 1745**

The Royal Court Theatre's
autumn season opens with
a new play by Terry Johnson

HYSTERIA

Freud, Salvador Dali, an ex-patient
and an elderly Jewish doctor meet
in Freud's London house with comic
consequences which could affect
the future of psycho-analysis.

from 23 august
Royal Court Theatre [071 730 1745]

11 - 16 october
Arts Centre, University of Warwick [0203 524524]

25 - 30 october
Theatre Royal, Richmond [081 940 0088]

1 - 6 november
Theatre Royal, Newcastle [091 232 2061]

Royal Court Theatre is a registered charity [number 231242]

THE LAST PLACE
ON EARTH

44

Editor: Bill Buford
Deputy Editor: Tim Adams
Managing Editor: Ursula Doyle
Editorial Assistant and Picture Researcher: Cressida Leyshon
Contributing Editor: Rose Kernochan

Managing Director: Catherine Eccles
Financial Controller: Geoffrey Gordon
Circulation Manager: Sally Lewis
Subscriptions Assistant: Tracy Urquhart
Office Assistant: Tania M. Almond

Picture Editor: Alice Rose George
Executive Editor: Pete de Bolla
US Publisher: Anne Kinard, Granta, 250 West 57th Street, Suite 1316, New York, NY 10107.

Editorial and Subscription Correspondence: Granta, 2–3 Hanover Yard, Noel Road, Islington, London N1 8BE. Telephone: (071) 704 9776. Fax: (071) 704 0474. Subscriptions: (071) 704 0470.
A one-year subscription (four issues) is £21.95 in Britain, £29.95 for the rest of Europe and £36.95 for the rest of the world.
All manuscripts are welcome but must be accompanied by a stamped, self-addressed envelope or they cannot be returned.

Granta is printed in the United States of America. The paper used in this publication meets the minimum requirements of American National Standard for Information Sciences—Permanence of Paper for Printed Library Materials, ANSI Z39.48-1984 ∞

Granta is published by Granta Publications Ltd and distributed by Penguin Books Ltd, Harmondsworth, Middlesex, England; Viking Penguin, a division of Penguin Books USA Inc, 375 Hudson Street, New York, NY 10014, USA; Penguin Books Australia Ltd, Ringwood, Victoria, Australia; Penguin Books Canada Ltd, 2801 John Street, Markham, Ontario, Canada L3R 1BR; Penguin Books (NZ) Ltd, 182–190 Wairau Road, Auckland 10, New Zealand. This selection copyright © 1993 by Granta Publications Ltd.

Cover by Senate. Photograph: Larry Sultan.

Granta 44
ISBN 0140 140 62X

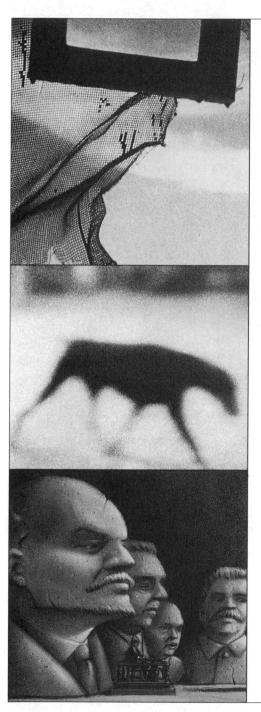

THE ENGLISH PATIENT
Michael Ondaatje

Winner of the 1992 Booker Prize

'Profound, beautiful and heart-quickening'
TONI MORRISON

£5.99

BLACK DOGS
Ian McEwan

'This is a brilliant book'
NEW YORKER

£4.99

THE PORCUPINE
Julian Barnes

'A masterpiece of political satire: compelling, funny and frightening'
ROBERT HARRIS

£4.99

flamingo   *Fine Writing*

A compelling literary ghost story...

A novel which will haunt you forever...

M John Harrison

THE COURSE OF THE HEART

16 AUGUST

'*Sheer brilliance*'
IAIN BANKS

'*A short, sharp shocker... reads like a cross between John Fowles and Iris Murdoch*'
INDEPENDENT ON SUNDAY

ALSO AVAILABLE IN FLAMINGO ORIGINAL PAPERBACK

Barbara Gowdy

WE SO SELDOM LOOK ON LOVE

16 AUGUST

'*Gowdy's is a talent that will make a major impact on what's left of the millennium*'
TORONTO STAR

Edward Toman

SHAMBLES CORNER

27 SEPTEMBER

'*Shambles Corner is extraordinary. The true personality of the Irish is captured in this book, harsh, proud, rebellious, sensitive, funny and, in turn, lovable*'
J P DONLEAVY

 An imprint of Harper Collins *Publishers*

Contents

Playing it Again

The Casablanca Man

The Cinema of Michael Curtiz

James C. Robertson

This first comprehensive critical exploration of Curtiz's entire career, treating his European work and his subsequent American work as a coherent whole, firmly establishes Curtiz's true standing in the history of cinema.

June 1993: 234x156: 208pp: illus. 14 b+w   Hb: £25.00

Theatre and the World

Performance and the Politics of Culture

Rustom Bharucha

What are the ethics of post-colonial representation? In this passionate and controversial work, Rustom Bharucha presents the first major critique of intercultural theatre from a 'Third World' perspective.

July 1993: 234x156: 272pp   Hb: £35.00   Pb: £12.99

The Colonial Rise of the Novel

Firdous Azim

'An exceptionally powerful contribution to post-colonial criticism... A major intervention in debates about the epistemological underpinnings of the Western novel.'
- Joseph Bristow, University of York

September 1993: 216x138: 240pp   Hb: £35.00   Pb: £10.99

Marguerite Duras

Apocalyptic Desires

Leslie Hill

'Hill takes us into the heartlands of Duras' self-promotional mythology and analyses her work in a variety of media with astonishing dexterity and confidence.'
- Malcolm Bowie, University of Oxford

July 1993: 234x156: 272pp
Hb: £35.00   Pb: £12.99

Available through booksellers.
For further information please
contact: James Powell,
Routledge, 11 New Fetter Lane
London EC4P 4EE.
Tel: 071 583 9855

ROUTLEDGE

GRANTA

TRACY KIDDER
THE LAST PLACE ON EARTH

Linda Manor

Inside, the corridors brighten. The living-room windows begin to reflect the lights on the plastic Christmas tree, and the view through those windows is fading, the woods growing thicker, the birches glowing in the dusk. At the end of the long corridor, a white-haired woman in a plain housedress and sneakers leans against a radiator, a cane in her hands, and she gazes out at clouds. She is very forgetful and yet very nostalgic and, of all the people who live here, the most devoted to windows. 'They come and go,' she says of the clouds. 'I guess that's to be expected. First they're dark and then they're light. First they're there and then they're gone.' She makes a small laugh. She goes on gazing through the glass. 'I don't know what all this business is about, living this way. I tried to figure it out, but I can't.' The clouds hovering above the silhouette of the far ridge are sharply etched, clouds of the north wind, dark grey in the last light of a sky still too bright for stars.

The light seeps away. The windows throw back watery images of carpeted corridors that could belong to a clean motel. It is night. Lou Freed comes out of his room, just past the elevators. Lou is small and plump in the middle, with fleecy white hair and thick, dark-framed glasses. The lid of his left eye droops. His close-cropped moustache is a dash of white across his face. His forehead and cheeks are deeply furrowed. Lou wears a look of concentration. He holds a cane in his right hand, its black shaft striped like a barber pole with yellowish tape. Lou applied the tape several years ago when his eyes began to fail and he couldn't cross a street very quickly any more. He used to hold the cane aloft as he crossed, hoping it would catch the attention of drivers. He no longer has to worry about crossing streets, but he's left the tape in place.

Lou leans on his cane, but not heavily. He walks with his legs spread well apart, his left arm swinging free and a little away from his torso, while his right arm works the cane. He crosses the corridor and then turns south, following the carpet's border, travelling in a slow, sturdy gait, like an old sailor on a rolling deck, passing along a wall equipped with an oak handrail and adorned with cream-coloured wallpaper and rose-coloured mouldings, framed prints of flowers, puppies and English hunting scenes.

The nurses' station, enclosed within a formica counter, is brightly lit as always. Lou stops at the corner. He shifts his cane to his left hand and slides his right hand up the wall, until it touches the edge of a four-gang light switch. His fingers are nimble. They move with a confident inquisitiveness, but fumble slightly over the plate of the light switch. This isn't the switch that Lou wants. He finds the one he wants by finding this one first. His hand pauses here tonight, however. The plastic plate surrounding one of these four switches feels warm. In Lou's experience, this sometimes signifies a circuit overload. Nothing serious, but he'll have to remember to tell Bruce, the director of maintenance, tomorrow.

Lou's hand moves on, across the wall, fingers fumbling again, until they strike a two-gang switch. Then with a flick of the forefinger, joyous in its certainty, Lou throws both switches up and night-lights come on in all of the bedrooms on the floor.

Night-lights are important. They might save other residents from falling on the way to their bathrooms in the dark. April, one of the aides, has forgotten to turn them on. Or else she's been too busy. When that happens, Lou does the job. He doesn't mind. It is a job.

'Hi, Lou.' A nurse, a young woman in slacks—the nurses here don't wear uniforms—stands nearby, behind the medication cart, studying her records.

'Hi,' Lou says. 'Who's that?'

'Eileen,' she says, adding, 'Lou, did you get your iron today?'

Lou smiles. His arms are thin. The flesh sags from them. But when he lifts his right arm and makes as if to flex his bicep, some muscle rises. 'Pretty soon I'll be sweating rust.' Lou has a soft, gravelly voice.

The nurse chuckles. Lou smiles. Then he shifts his cane to his right hand, his face grows serious again and he starts slowly back down the carpeted hallway towards his room. As Lou nears the doorway, he hears the sound of screeching tyres. He enters to the sounds of gunfire.

The lights are out and the curtains drawn. Lou's room-mate, Joe Torchio, lies on his back on the bed near the door, a bald-headed, round-faced, round-bellied man. In the changeable glow of his television, Joe looks beached and bristly. Lou feels his way past Joe to the other side of the room and begins to get ready for bed. The charge nurse knocks. Joe flicks his remote control at the television, leaving it lit but mute, and the nurse enters, carrying pills.

Back in his eighties, Lou knew all the names and functions of his medicines. Now he takes too many to remember, though he still makes inquiries about the new ones now and then. Joe has said he doesn't know what pills the nurses give him and he doesn't care. 'If they want to kill me, go ahead,' Joe likes to say, and Lou replies, 'Joe, don't talk that way.' Lou says he isn't worried, because the pills he takes all have arrows on them to tell them where to go once they get inside. The nurse laughs: Lou and Joe may take a lot of pills, but they are among the healthiest of Linda Manor's residents.

Joe turns and looks at Lou, who has now climbed into his bed. 'We're the best!' Joe exclaims.

'God help the others if we're the best,' Lou says.

'Anyway, I can't read.'

'I could read if I could see.'

'I have half a brain, and you can't see,' Joe says.

'And so betwixt us both, we licked the platter clean,' Lou says. He smiles, the covers pulled up to his chin, and he sighs. 'Ahh dear. It's a great life, if you don't weaken.'

Joe aims his remote control at his television. The sounds of a car chase resume, and Lou drifts off to sleep.

It seemed so new a place for people so old. Linda Manor opened for business only a little more than a year ago. It stood in what had been a hayfield, in a suburban-bucolic setting on Route 9, a few miles west of downtown Northampton, Massachusetts. It had balconies and railings along its flat roofs and wide frieze boards under its eaves. There was a portico, supported on four Doric columns, and two tall flag-poles, and a little fountain, like a child's wading pool. And everything, except for the brick walls, was painted white. The building looked not quite finished, like the parts of a giant wedding cake laid side to side.

The obligation of finding a nursing home for a sick, aged person usually falls to a daughter. On any given day in the region, a middle-aged woman would be looking around for an acceptable establishment. There were a few. But there were also places where the stench of urine got in one's clothes like tobacco smoke, where four, sometimes five, elderly people lay jammed in tiny rooms, where residents sat tied to wheelchairs and strapped to beds, where residents weren't allowed to bring any furniture of their own or have private phones or use the public pay phone without nurses listening in. One woman, on a recent tour of a nearby place, had been shown a room with a dead resident in it.

Linda Manor had some unusually pleasant qualities. The staff wasn't the largest per resident in the area but large by the usual standards and far larger than the state required. Every room got natural light. There was a small greenhouse. Residents were allowed to have their own telephones. No one was to be tied up or doped into insensibility, at least not as a matter of covert procedure. This policy of 'no restraints' was very rare in the world of nursing homes. The local newspaper carried a long story about it when Linda Manor first opened. The publicity helped to make the policy work. A good reputation meant lots of applications for beds. The management could afford to turn away the very violent and most floridly demented.

New residents arrived from hospitals mainly, and occasionally from other nursing homes. Some arrived directly from their own or their children's homes, and for them the transition tended to come hardest. A few died within days of arriving, one on her very first day, and it was hard to resist a Victorian explanation, that they had died of broken hearts. More often, though, the health of new residents stabilized or even improved. Some residents merely stopped here, to rest and receive a few months of therapy on the way home from the hospital. One well-heeled, well-travelled, well-read woman declared, soon after arriving, that she never played bingo in her life and did not intend to start now. She stayed at Linda Manor for a year, read most of Proust and then returned home. But hers was a very unusual case.

By this time, December 1990, Linda Manor was running at capacity—121 beds, all full—although its grounds were often empty. Their quietude lent a secretive quality to the sprawling, low-roofed building—set back from busy Route 9, surrounded by wintry woods and dormant grass as white as a nurse's starched uniform. As one stared at it, the place grew odder in the mind. The building looked so provisional. So new and yet containing so much of the past. Many residents remembered World War One as if it ended yesterday. Some remembered first-hand accounts of the Civil War. They were like immigrants arriving in a new land with long lives behind them, obliged to inhabit a place that was bound to seem less real than the places they remembered. For most of those long-lived, ailing people, Linda Manor represented all the permanence that life still had to offer. It was their home for the duration, their last place on earth.

Lou

Lou and Joe had become room-mates.

Lou had come to Linda Manor with his ailing wife Jennie. They had been married for almost seventy years when Jennie died, in early March of 1989. In the weeks afterwards, Lou walked the familiar corridors of Linda Manor on his cane. For hours at a time, he sat alone in the room he'd shared with Jennie, where the two beds, which Lou had once shoved together, now stood apart.

Jewish ritual prescribes that the period of mourning should last for thirty days of outward abstinence from joy. This was easy for Lou. He faced a new life, which consisted mainly of absences. He had thought of himself as his wife's main nurse and protector. Now he lacked his life's companion, and he lacked employment for the first time in eighty years. His daughter Ruth was very worried. She thought that Lou might find that there was nothing more for him to do, except to await an end. And an end wasn't clearly in sight. Lou was ninety, but bodies keep their own time.

A lot of men would say that their wives were their best friends, but Lou's wife really had been his. He hadn't lived in close quarters with another man since the army, more than seventy years ago. 'I don't know what it is to have a room-mate,' Lou thought. But although he'd never had a very close male friend, Lou had been on friendly terms with many men over the years. He used to meet a lot of new people in his work. He reminded himself that he'd made many new acquaintances at meetings of the Power Maintenance

14

Group of south New Jersey. This shouldn't be too hard.

With help from the maintenance men and his daughter Ruth, Lou furnished his side of his new room, the side near the window. Joe's bed was near the door. Lou then proceeded to equip his new resting place like an Egyptian tomb. He screwed a hook into his bedside dresser for his shoehorn. In the top drawer of his dresser, he constructed a tape-and-cardboard partition for his nitroglycerine pills so that he could find them at once without fumbling if he had angina in the night. He put his little kit of scissors, pliers and screwdrivers in there as well. In a corner by the window, he placed the four-legged walker that his wife Jennie used before she went into a wheelchair. Lou hung his striped cane from the walker's rung, also his blue machinist's apron, which he wore to meals because, in his near blindness, he sometimes spilled his food. He placed his push-button phone—it had oversize buttons—on top of his bedside dresser.

Lou placed a straight-backed armchair in front of the window, where the morning sun would warm his back, and covered the walls around him with old and recent family photos. Although the room was functional and drab—its floor a pale grey linoleum tile; its furniture all institutional, with photo-wood-grain finish—Lou covered most of the surfaces around him with cards and books and various knick-knacks. He kept his photo albums in a stack beside his radio. Sometimes he asked his daughter to read the captions beneath the photos in the albums. 'So I can sit here and think back,' he explained.

Joe's side of the room looked barren compared to Lou's. One time a visitor from Pittsfield brought Joe an old friend's obituary. Joe kept it for a day. Then Lou heard him crumple it up and saw him toss it in the waste-basket. Lou wondered why Joe didn't keep it.

But Lou had begun to wonder quite a lot about his new room-mate, and as the weeks went by, he started to build up a picture. He decided that Joe was 'average size'; that is, about as tall as Lou, about as tall as most men used to be, about five-eight. Lou heard Joe say that he had to get his moustache trimmed, so he knew that Joe had acquired facial hair. In fact, the more Lou learned about Joe's personality, the more Joe puzzled him.

Joe mentioned having trouble with his bowels, in a voice full of mock-daintiness, saying, 'I have a lot of trouble with my e-elimination. I have a lot of trouble with my stools.'

Lou suggested prunes.

Soon Joe was eating about a dozen prunes for breakfast, but almost nothing else. Joe said that, among other things, he had diabetes and was afraid that if he gained more weight he'd end up having to take insulin by injection, and by God he'd rather die than that. That made sense, but once Lou learned the details of Joe's weight control programme, he began saying privately to his daughter that his new room-mate did 'some things that don't add up.'

He would go out to lunch—his family took him out once a week—come back and say, 'Oh, dear God, I ate too much.' He would heave himself on to his bed, and add, 'It was worth it.' The next day Joe would weigh himself and fume. 'Jesus Christ! I gained a pound.' He'd go on a diet, eating little more than prunes for the rest of the week, which Lou thought must be insufficient for a diabetic. After breakfast they'd come back upstairs to the room. Lou would sit by the window and then hear a ripping sound. Joe was undoing the velcro straps of his orthopaedic shoes. A clattering followed, the sound of the steel brace attached to Joe's right shoe hitting the floor. And then Joe's bed would creak, which signified that he was lying down again. He always lay down when he came into the room and hardly ever budged from there between meals. And then he wondered why he had trouble with his weight.

Lou himself didn't get as much exercise as he thought he should. He used to take Jennie out for walks, pushing her wheelchair around the corridors. He didn't walk as often now. 'I don't have the incentive,' he said. But then, feeling slothful, he would get up from his chair, take his cane and walk across the room and out the door. He'd cross the hall, touch the wall on the other side and then return. Sometimes he'd do several laps before he resettled himself in his chair. And three mornings a week he went downstairs to the physical therapy room for the formal sessions of gentle exercise and stretching called 'Music and Motion'—'M&Ms' for short. All the exercises were performed while sitting down. It was a pretty good workout, Lou said, touting M&Ms to Joe. Joe would benefit from M&Ms. Maybe he just needed encouragement. So, on one M&Ms morning, Lou said towards the shape of Joe, 'Why don't you come down with me?'

But Joe said he didn't feel like it.

Joe was watching a baseball game on his television, and the room was filled with the folksy voices of Boston Red Sox play-by-play announcers, and with the louder sounds Joe made while watching—shouts of joy sometimes and, at least as often, strings of oaths, as Joe thundered at the Red Sox manager, 'Jesus Christ! Goddamn it! I told you not to put him in! Jesus Christ!'

Lou was amused. He could not imagine getting that emotionally involved in baseball, but this was not as strange as Joe's other tendencies. A young nurse's aide came into the room to check their vitals, and Joe questioned her about the intimate facts of her life. Was she married? Did she have any kids? She had two and another one on the way. Three children were enough, Joe told her. 'Tell your husband. Vasa-sectomy! Snip, snip, snip,' said Joe.

Joe was laughing when he said that, but he always grilled the staff. 'You married? You living with someone? Why the hell don't you marry him?' One of the staff said she'd gotten a dog. 'Did you worm it yet?' Joe wanted to know. And there were any number of nurses and aides—Lou couldn't say just how many, because he couldn't tell all of their voices apart—who, under Joe's questioning, revealed that they had trouble collecting alimony. Joe told them how to go after their ex-husbands. Sometimes he gave them names of people to call. Joe had been a probation officer. Maybe he was trying to keep his hand in.

And then there was Joe on the telephone. He called his wife every evening. At the end, he said, 'OK, we'll see ya,' and hung up. He always hung up that way, sounding peremptory and gruff.

One evening he called his son and got the answering machine. Joe growled into the phone. 'This is your father. Jesus Christ!'

It sounded to Lou as if Joe had said, 'This is your father, Jesus Christ.' Lou had to make an effort to keep from laughing out loud. He wasn't sure how Joe would react. It wasn't worth the risk. It might make him angrier. If Joe got any angrier, Lou thought, he might keel over with a stroke.

For all of that, Joe was turning out to be good company. He had a sense of humour and liked hearing stories. Lou never felt as if Joe's anger was aimed at him. 'He gets angry, but he doesn't really mean it,' Lou thought. He wasn't frightened of Joe, just puzzled.

Night baseball games began. Then Lou went to sleep to the mingled sounds of play-by-play and his room-mate's half-stifled cheers and curses. Almost daily, it seemed, Joe said, 'I weighed myself, Jesus Christ! It's impossible! I don't eat!'

Lou could not resist offering a little advice; the solution seemed so near at hand. Lou said again, 'Why don't you come down to M&Ms with me?'

All right, Joe said. He'd try it.

Joe

Joe was gazing out the picture window, at the view of field and woods, very leafy, very green. He'd been working outside on a hot day just before his stroke, almost twenty years ago. The picture window was now closed against the heat. Joe lay on his back. He had been telling Lou about the missing big toe on his partially paralysed right foot. After the surgeon cut it off, he asked what Joe wanted done with it. 'I told him, "Why don't you sent it to Chicago and have it bronzed? I'll put it on my mantelpiece." For God's sake.'

Lou smiled.

But, said Joe, he wished he'd told the surgeon to wrap it up and send it to a certain judge in Pittsfield, the one who forced him into retirement about eight years ago.

Lou could understand how a person might hold a grudge, but, he said, he couldn't think of any he had held himself. Except once—against a company that wouldn't give him a job because he was a Jew. But he got even. While running the pen factory, Lou said, he had the opportunity to tell one of that company's salesmen that he wouldn't do business with him. And that squared matters, as far as Lou was concerned.

Some of the things Lou said surprised Joe.

Lou said he dated only one girl, and he married her.

Joe said he dated many, and none ever dumped him.

Lou said that back during Prohibition he built a still for a relative, but didn't drink any of the alcohol, because that would have been illegal. Actually, Lou said, he got drunk only once in his life. 'Did I tell you that story?' he asked Joe.

Lou sometimes repeated stories. But Lou was an old man, Joe told himself. He had already heard this story, but he didn't say anything, and Lou told again how on his birthday years ago he went to a nightclub called The Stable, in Philadelphia, and had about three beers. 'I suddenly felt something I never felt before. I was spinning around. I excused myself and went across the street to a drugstore and got some Alka Seltzer.'

Joe guffawed. 'Three beers. That isn't drunk! I used to *drink*. Good God.'

Lou said he'd never smoked. He believed in moderation.

Joe had smoked most of his life. He smiled at the ceiling. 'Moderation I was never for.'

Lou said that he grew up in tough, seamy parts of Philadelphia. 'I sometimes wonder, growing up where I did, why I didn't get in more trouble.'

But Joe had worked with people who got in trouble. Lou's stories made it obvious that Lou had never gotten into anything like trouble.

On Saturday mornings, the phone rang for Lou constantly. All of his relatives called. Joe turned down his TV, so Lou could talk, which meant that Joe could not help overhearing. 'I love you,' Lou said into the phone every time, before hanging up. Every time! Wasn't there anyone in Lou's family Lou didn't love? Was there anyone in the world this old man didn't like?

They got talking about their wives.

Lou told of how Jennie suffered from skin irritations before her death. She was incontinent, and Lou figured out that the nurse's aides made up her bed all wrong for a person in her condition— with a plastic sheet beneath her sheet instead of absorbent pads. He showed them how to do it right, and, his soft voice suddenly loud and stern, admitted that he had to struggle with the staff sometimes to make sure that Jennie got proper attention. The staff worked hard and most were good. Lou often praised them. But one time he found Jennie wet and set off every call-bell in their room, and no one came. So he grabbed his cane and marched down to the nurse's station. 'I could see a little better then.' On the other side of the counter, he saw the hazy shapes of aides and nurses, all in a group, and the figure of a man addressing them. The man had to be a doctor. Evidently the staff thought a doctor's words of wisdom more important than call-bells. Evidently the doctor thought so, too. Lou slapped his hand hard on the counter and yelled at them. 'Jennie needs attention! And she needs it *now*!' Lou's countenance was stern, recalling this. 'And I got results.'

More softly, Lou said, 'I still wish I'd gone with her. But I thank the good Lord I didn't have to leave her alone.'

Joe listened, gazing intently at the ceiling. Joe listed his own wife's many ailments. 'I wore her out. She couldn't take care of me any more, that's all.'

Lou said that he and Jennie never went to sleep without kissing first.

'Well, I did!' said Joe. 'Because we'd argue, and she wouldn't talk to me.'

'I don't think I ever had an argument with Jennie,' said Lou. He and his wife had disagreements, but never went to bed without settling them first, and kissing.

Joe sat up in bed and stared at Lou. 'Jesus Christ! That's impossible!'

Lou was too much. It sometimes seemed as if he must have lived in an entirely different world from the one that Joe had known. And yet they had a certain amount of history in common. Lou's parents were immigrants from Austria, and Joe's father was a shoemaker from Calabria. Joe, too, grew up in a largely immigrant neighbourhood, on Pittsfield's Dewey Avenue. Lou grew up within walking distance of burlesque shows and whorehouses, while it was said of Joe's high school that the graduates either became judges or bank robbers. But all of Lou's father's business ventures failed, while Joe's father's business, Artistic Shoe Renovator, prospered modestly during the Depression, when many people got their shoes repaired instead of buying new ones. Joe's parents had been able to send him to college. As a consequence Joe was much more widely read.

There were deep differences, too.

Lou said he loved the Horatio Alger rags-to-riches books as a boy, and later on the poems of Robert Service. Joe had wider, less sunny tastes in literature. The kind of poem he didn't like was one he used to hear recited and could still recite in part himself. 'Grow old along with me. The best is yet to be,' Joe chanted. 'When I was thirty, forty, I thought it was all right. But now, bullshit, it's false.' One of his favourite poems—it lay in the anthology that Joe had carried with him across the Pacific in the navy—was Stephen Crane's 'The Wayfarer'.

The wayfarer,
Perceiving the pathway to truth,
Was struck with astonishment.
It was thickly grown with weeds.
'Ha,' he said,
'I see that none has passed here
In a long time.'
Later he saw that each weed
Was a singular knife.
'Well,' he mumbled at last,
'Doubtless there are other roads.'

Joe smiled wryly over that poem. '*Doubtless* there are other roads.'

'I quit lying in my thirties,' Joe said once. Then he amended that statement. 'I quit lying about everything *except* drinking.'

Lou told again about that time when he'd gotten drunk. 'I can remember the place. Place called The Stable. I never felt I missed something.'

'Well,' said Joe, 'you missed something.'

'I saw enough people that way that I never wanted to be that way myself,' said Lou from his chair over by the window.

'I saw a lot of people get drunk and got drunk myself,' Joe said, lying on his bed.

'I enjoyed life without getting drunk,' Lou said.

Joe's voice softened. 'It made it easier on the people close to you.'

Most cynical and pessimistic utterances seemed to leave Lou

21

truly puzzled, not naïvely so, but puzzled as to why some people chose to think that way. One time when Lou's daughter Ruth was visiting, she said that she had a Ph.D. in guilt, and Lou said, 'I don't think I feel guilty about anything.' And Joe thought to himself again, 'Jesus Christ, that's impossible.' If in the privacy of their room, Joe made a little sport of a fellow resident, Lou might join in, but he would usually end up saying, 'Poor soul. We shouldn't laugh.' And then, if one of those people got sick and was confined to bed, Lou would go and pay a visit. Perhaps Lou did dislike some people after all. He sometimes talked as if he did. 'But,' Joe thought, 'it has to be a very mean man.'

After his experiences with other room-mates, Joe hadn't relished the idea of a ninety-year-old moving in with him. Being only seventy-two himself and burdened with a textbook's worth of ailments, Joe had figured that by ninety there couldn't be much left of a person. But Joe now had to remind himself how old, really old, Lou was. The man sometimes seemed too virtuous to be true, but he clearly wasn't senile. 'He's got all his buttons, by Jesus,' Joe thought. He felt grateful for that.

Thanksgiving

Both Lou and Joe packed overnight bags and went away for Thanksgiving, Lou to his daughter Ruth's house and Joe back to his former home in Pittsfield. Lou returned feeling all worn out. For him, trips away had become exhausting. 'I don't know what the problem is. Too many birthdays, I guess.'

Joe limped back to their room, saying that there had been too much company back home. He'd had to retreat to his old den at times. Joe also weighed a few pounds more than when he'd left. This didn't surprise Lou, nor did the consequences. Lou had inspired Joe to exercise, which included not only M&Ms, but daily rides on the stationary bike. Every time Joe rode, he pedalled further and faster. And so now, to work off Thanksgiving, he went straight back to the bike. Then, on an afternoon a few days later, after an especially vigorous ride, a blister erupted on the big toe of Joe's left foot, his good foot.

It was a little blue capsule with some red at the edges, the kind of blister that weekend carpenters raise on their thumbs. As soon as the nurse's aide saw it she summoned the charge nurse, and the nurse put in a call to Joe's doctor, who made a special visit. He put Joe on an antibiotic.

Diabetes reduces circulation. Even Joe's relatively mild case made his toes, because of their distance from his heart, especially vulnerable to infection and the risk of dread gangrene. This blister, like a broken hip, could lead to graver complications. Out of Lou and Joe's hearing, a nurse remarked, 'Joe could lose the toe.' Whether Joe's body or his spirits could withstand another blow like that was an open question. Lou knew the blister must be serious if it had caused a doctor to make a special visit here. And a parade of aides and nurses kept coming in to have a look at Joe's toe. After listening to the commotion for a time, Lou got up, fetched his cane from the corner, and, saying to Joe that he guessed he'd take a walk, made his way to the elevator, rode downstairs and walked down the long central corridor until he reached the door of his favourite nursing supervisor. She had been helpful in Jennie's last days. Lou knocked on the door with the handle of his cane. 'Kathleen?'

'Yes, Lou?'

'Kathleen, I'd like you to take a look at Joe's toe.'

They discussed the blister, and she said she'd come and look at it. Lou thanked her, then made his way, by cane and handrail and carpet border, back upstairs to his chair by the window.

Kathleen had told Lou that Joe's blister would almost certainly heal, and Lou believed her. The nursing care was good in here. If a person came down with something curable, a lot of the staff acted as if they'd been given a present. But why take chances? Joe shouldn't go downstairs for meals for a while, Lou decided. Lou told Joe he should take it easy, stay up here and keep his foot elevated.

But Joe wouldn't hear of it. 'The hell with it,' Joe said.

It was a few days after the blister had appeared. Lou sat by the window, warming his back in the morning sun, and said to Joe, '*Eigueshpart*. Stubborn.' Joe lay as usual on his bed, but with his wounded foot propped up on a pillow. 'That's what you were on that bicycle, Joe.'

23

A curtain hung from tracks in the ceiling. Joe sat up and pulled it back so he could confront Lou directly. 'No, I wasn't!'

'Yes. I told you you were overdoing it.'

Joe lay back and grunted at the ceiling.

Lou smiled. The low December sun suffused his white hair, as if through a thin, fleecy cloud. 'You guys don't listen to me. After all, Joe, stop and think about it. I'm old enough to be your father.'

'I know it!' Joe laughed. Then his right arm went into a jackhammer-like shaking. With his left hand, Joe grasped the wrist of the shivering arm and pulled it over on to his stomach, and it stopped. He gazed at the ceiling again.

Since Lou became a room-mate, Joe was getting out a little more. He now went to bingo, three times a week. Lou went to most scheduled activities *except* bingo. On Sundays they both looked forward to a television show that carried them off to other parts of the country—Joe watching and Lou listening. Tuesday morning they both went to Literary Hour, when Lou's daughter Ruth, who was a retired high school English teacher, read aloud to residents in the activity room.

Ruth visited every morning, seven days a week. And even though she had an incentive to like Linda Manor—not many people can bear to feel their parent's nursing home is bad—she knew it was a decent place. A faint odour like buttered toast, with the butter a little off, lingered in parts of the building, and Ruth sometimes caught the sharp whiff of urine, but on the whole Linda Manor was remarkably odourless. As for its sights and sounds, Ruth had long since grown accustomed to them. It was the vision of the life to come that got her down. The visible decline of residents who came to her Literary Hour—that woman who seemed so sprightly last week on her cane, appearing this week in a wheelchair, bravely trying to smile; or the nearly comatose laid out in their bedrooms; the demented wandering the halls. Once, on her way out, she was approached by a nice-looking resident who asked if she would please give him a ride home. She left in tears, feeling sorry for the man and for the fact that her own father now resided among people who seemed consigned to live no life at all.

'Guilt's my middle name,' Ruth said. It was entirely self-inflicted. Lou often reminded her that he'd rather live here than at her home, where inevitably he'd be alone and bored. He was always telling her that she didn't have to come every day, urging her to go away with her husband. But now, when she and her husband were both retired and in good health and had the money to travel, she couldn't tear herself away. She once took a trip to England and felt miserable the whole time. She made herself busy, taking courses and doing charitable work. She felt that what she did had to be arduous and important to justify keeping Lou here. Maybe if he had turned into a querulous old man, insisting that she visit him every day, it would have been possible for her not to do so, or at least feel that she was being dutiful enough. His cheerfulness intensified her 'guilt spasms'.

A nursing home proceeds to many different clocks. Time in Lou and Joe's room became the time of the blister on Joe's toe. It was marked by the judicious looks and noncommittal words of the nurses, and by Joe's growing weariness with the question, 'How's the blister, Joe?'

He still could not return to M&Ms or ride the exercise bike. But he couldn't resist weighing himself each morning. 'Good God. I gained a pound,' Joe said, lying on his back on his bed. 'I think it was the jello last night.'

'I don't think so,' Lou said, from his chair by the window. 'When you were bicycling like mad, you weren't losing weight.'

'I wasn't bicycling like mad,' Joe said. But his voice wasn't vehement. What was the sense of arguing? Lou was right, and Joe might as well admit it.

'Yes, you were,' said Lou. 'I told you you were going at it too hard. Like do or die.'

Joe gazed up at the ceiling. 'That's right. *Eigueshpart.* Well, I paid for it. Two weeks and it won't heal.'

Joe missed the bike. 'It made my leg feel *strong*, you know.' But everyone here had problems of one sort or another, most much worse than this. The blister would pass, Joe told himself. Days ran into each other. Life in the room wasn't all that different, really. To be here at all was to be laid up. Joe was just a little more laid up for now.

He and Lou could not control most of the substance of their life, but they had imposed a style on it. The way for instance that he and Lou had come to deal with matters of the bathroom, where Joe seemed to have to go a ridiculous number of times—day and night. He and Lou referred to the bathroom as 'the library'. The mock-daintiness of the term amused Joe. Up in the room after breakfast, Joe would say to Lou, 'I gotta go to the library. I have to do my, uh, uh, prune evacuation.'

The staff talked quite frankly about matters of Lou and Joe's biology. Too frankly for Lou. Too frankly for Joe, once Lou had made the point. The aides, 'the girls', used to come to the doorway, cradling the large, ledger-like 'BM Book' in their arms, and they'd call loudly in, 'Did either of you gentlemen have a bowel movement today?' It was Lou, some months ago, who responded by telling the girls gently: 'All you have to say is, "Did you or didn't you?"' The way Lou did that impressed Joe, so much more diplomatically than Joe would have.

It was a morning in December, in the third week of Joe's blister. Joe had the television news on. He wasn't waiting for the aide with the BM Book, but he had a question ready for her. When the aide came to the door, she asked, 'For my book. Did you?'

'Yes.' Joe tilted his head towards Lou. 'And so did he.' Then, a little smile blossoming, Joe looked at the aide and asked, 'And what about you?'

'None of your business!' The aide looked embarrassed. She laughed.

'Well, you ask me,' Joe said.

'But I get paid for it.'

'Goodbye,' Joe said pleasantly, and went back to watching the news.

Joe's doctor changed Joe's antibiotic. Probably that did the trick, or maybe time deserved the credit. In any case, Joe awoke one morning near the end of December and for a moment he couldn't see the blister. So Joe was cleared for a return to M&Ms and stationary biking. But when Lou asked, 'You coming down to M&Ms?' Joe said he didn't feel like it today.

With Joe it was all or nothing, Lou thought. Lou shook his

head. 'He's his own worst enemy.' In the afternoon, contemplating the shape of Joe, lying over there, Lou had an idea. He got up and fetched his cane. 'Joe, I'm going out for a walk.' But that didn't work. Joe didn't get the hint.

Lou understood the problem. You get old and you get rusty. You go without exercise for a while, and you don't feel like exercising any more. But persistence had worked on Joe before. Lou figured it would work again. He'd just keep asking the question, until Joe got sick of it. 'Joe, why don't you come down to M&Ms with me tomorrow?'

'All right,' Joe said finally. He didn't sound too happy about it, but he would be, Lou thought.

A little later, Lou went off alone downstairs. Just to take a walk, he told Joe. Actually, Lou went to the physical therapy room, searching for the voice of Carol, the physical therapy aide who ran M&Ms and supervised Joe's biking.

The next morning all was just as it had been before Joe's blister. Joe limped into the physical therapy room and took his usual seat, an armchair next to Lou's. Carol welcomed Joe back. She told him she had attached some foam-rubber pads to the pedals of the bike. That way Joe could ride in his stockinged feet, lessening the chance of another blister.

'It was an extra thing for you to do,' Joe said to Carol. 'Thank you.'

'Well, I just wanted you to be able to use the bike again,' Carol said. She paused, and then added, 'But maybe not quite so violently.'

As she said these words, Carol glanced at Lou.

Joe's eyes followed Carol's to Lou. Lou was making an effort to look completely nonchalant. It showed. Joe smiled.

New Year's Eve

The New Year's Eve celebration started at two p.m. in order to accommodate the nursing home's routines and the residents' bedtimes. A four-man combo, with drums, saxophone, accordion and bass guitar, set up its music stands in the wide doorway to the dining room. Crêpe-paper streamers stretched in webs among the chandeliers, and party favours lay with every table setting. At Linda Manor's parties, there was always a broad dichotomy between bustle and passivity, with the aides and managers dressed in party hats, waiting on the tables, blowing party horns and clacking party noise-makers, singing brassily along to the music; while many residents sat quietly with open mouths or smiling or looking grumpy. Now and then a nurse slipped in among the crowd, with a pill-cup in one hand and a water-cup in the other, and knelt down before a resident.

The combo was entirely white-haired. All four musicians looked as old as many of the residents. But age creates great biological disparities, far greater than differences at birth. Facing a room full of parked wheelchairs and walkers, of backs bent by osteoporosis, of ankles swollen, of renal insufficiency and heart disease, and of residents with vacant-looking faces holding stuffed animals in their laps, the elderly musicians in their ties and jackets seemed positively lively.

The combo warmed up with a few polkas and then switched to old dance hall numbers.

As the vocalist crooned, a woman with limbs of concentration camp thinness, bent forward, trying doggedly to work a sock over one of her shoes. There were those with vigorous minds but ruined bodies, such as Winifred, arrayed in her wheelchair, singing along. And others with ruined minds but vigorous bodies, such as grey-haired Zita, wandering aimlessly around the dining-room but with a spryness that Winifred and Lou and Joe could recapture only in their memories.

Lou and Joe had sat apart from the other residents. During a lull in the music, someone said loudly, 'These songs make me cry,' and Lou got up from his chair at once and groped his way to the door. Joe followed at a little distance and stopped, watching as Lou walked slowly down the administrative corridor. Lou was heading for the lobby. Joe wouldn't follow him.

Joe knew that Lou was thinking about his wife. Lou would probably go to the lobby and cry quietly, or if one of the staff stopped to talk to him, Lou might tell her about his wife's death and, his voice thin and wailing, say, 'I held her hand right up until the end. That's the way we started, and that's the way we ended up.' And afterwards, Lou would probably say to his listener, 'I think that little talk did me some good.'

Lou and Joe had discussed the issue of male crying. They agreed there was no shame in it. But Lou did not often cry in front of Joe. Perhaps that was because his crying was apt to make Joe cry, too. But Joe, no matter what he said, clearly did not like to cry in front of another man.

The so-called 'labile' tendency that accompanies many strokes had lingered for eighteen years in Joe. It made him feel like weeping over inconsequential things, such as the sight of a young tree growing. Even the news of an ugly gas station being torn down could make him cry, Joe said. His fits were brief but powerful-looking. He'd sob silently, often without tears, his mouth open and his shoulders shaking, a momentary, dry-heaving kind of sob. Then he'd run his good hand downward over his face and reappear unruffled-looking, sometimes smiling. The combo's old dance hall songs were strong stimuli, and Joe had wanted to get away before he was overwhelmed. Joe couldn't prevent weepiness, but he'd get out of public places if he could when the fit was on him—just as he would make sure to wipe the numbed right side of his mouth periodically, in case spittle that he couldn't feel had collected there.

Joe belonged to the generation whose young men felt compelled, even desperate, to join the military and serve in World War Two. Joe himself had searched for a military doctor who would overlook his congenital high blood pressure, although he then discovered war to be less glorious than advertised. But Joe absorbed his generation's ideal of manly virtue. He said he admired Hemingway for committing suicide, because suicide took courage. But if one chose to live on, one must weather one's own fate bravely, or at least without complaint.

The music wafted out of the activity room. This was Lou's first New Year's without his wife. Joe watched Lou move slowly towards the lobby. 'It's sad. Sad,' said Joe. He headed for the elevators, limping slowly. He had to stop to rest. When he made this short walk in the company of an able-bodied visitor or one of the nurses whom he advised on matters of alimony, Joe timed these halts with the conversation. He made it seem as if he stopped and leaned a while on his cane, simply in order to emphasize a point. Joe rode up to their room alone.

Earl

It was about two weeks later that Lou's daughter Ruth ran into an old acquaintance named Jean Duncan. Ruth had taught Jean's daughters in high school and asked after them. They were doing fine, but Jean's husband Earl was not. He had just arrived at Linda Manor—it was why Jean was here, too, visiting him—but he was very sick with heart trouble and feeling pretty low. Maybe Lou would visit Earl, Jean suggested. Earl needed a friend on the premises.

Ruth passed the message along, and Lou immediately set out for Earl's room.

In fact, Earl seemed a lot less depressed than advertised, Lou thought. Earl said he'd be going home soon. He asked Lou to call on him again. And so, a few mornings later, Lou headed off once again to perform what he called his *mitzvah*, his good deed for the day.

There were two beds in the room. Earl sat on the edge of the bed nearer the door. He wore a nightshirt. His grey hair was mussed and sticking up in back, like a cow-lick. A blue oxygen catheter had been looped over his ears and across his upper lip, like a long, thin handlebar moustache. His wrists were knobby. He was painfully thin. 'I'm sorry, Lou,' said Earl. He spoke rapidly, with a hint of nervous haste, the haste of a man short of breath. 'I'm sorry, Lou. I haven't been able to sleep at all. My bowels. I've got one of these on.'

Earl pulled up his nightshirt, revealing a disposable diaper wrapped around thin thighs.

'I can't see. What is it?' asked Lou.

'It's one of these . . . ' Earl started to say. 'Like a child's bib. Not a bib . . . ' Earl's voice trailed off. 'I'm going to try to go back to sleep, Lou. I'm sorry.'

'No need to apologize,' said Lou. 'I'll see ya later.' Lou added, 'Take it easy.'

'I will,' Earl said emphatically, swinging his legs back into bed.

Earl was obviously a newcomer. Among most of the men at Linda Manor, 'Take it easy' called for an answer like, 'At my age, you don't have any choice.' And Lou chuckled. Lou meant to express solidarity. His chuckle was strained, though.

Lou headed back down the corridors. A member of the staff, falling in step with Lou, told him, 'Earl might be dying now.'

Lou pursed his lips. He looked grim. 'That's what happens.' he said.

Mitzvahs didn't always turn out well. This one had left him thinking about Jennie. He was picturing her as she'd lain in their room, during that time that Lou called 'towards the end,' when she'd weighed all of eighty pounds and the staff could pick her up as if she were a child. His deeply-lined face slightly frowning, Lou said again, 'That's what happens.'

Earl rallied, not for the first time. A few days after Lou visited, Earl was sitting up on the edge of his bed, making notes about his family's history.

Earl grew up twenty miles from here in Holyoke, during that now impoverished city's industrial heyday. As a teenager he worked at the Farr Alpaca Mill and attended the Holyoke Evening High School. He was elected President of his night school class. Having started caddying at the age of eight, he discovered a talent for golf, which proved as useful as a diploma once he got into banking. 'A lot of wealthy men wanted to play with me,' he explained.

Earl retired, as a bank vice-president, at the age of sixty-five. He had by then compiled a long record of public service. On retirement, he added to it. He served at one time or another as president, secretary, treasurer, director, trustee or plain fund-raiser for a huge number of civic, professional and charitable organizations. He'd been president and director of the Holyoke Rotary, a director of the local Red Cross, a member of the board of the local chamber of commerce, a treasurer of the Tuberculosis Society, a chairman of the united Cerebral Palsy and the American Heart Association fund-raising campaigns, a treasurer, trustee and senior warden of the St Paul's Episcopal Church in Holyoke, a member of the Bishop's Council, a president and district governor of two banking organizations. The list went on and on. He even served on a committee dedicated to saving a beautiful old merry-go-round. It was the curriculum vitae of a man too gregarious and generous to say no.

Earl's first wife had died by the time he retired. In his sixties he married Jean, who was thirteen years younger, and he began a second life made of public service, golf, family and travel. Earl had mildly high blood pressure and mild diabetes mellitus, and, in his early seventies, he was operated on for prostate cancer. But those ailments all appeared to be in check. He felt wonderful and young, until on a day in July in his seventy-ninth year, the day after playing in a golf tournament, Earl went to Cooley Dickinson Hospital in Northampton for his routine quarterly cancer check-up. He had a deep, dull pain in his chest. He felt nauseous. He told the receptionist he didn't feel up to having a check-up and was on his way out the door when he decided he'd better find out what was wrong. Earl later said—no doubt correctly—that he probably would have died if he hadn't turned back. In almost no time at all, he was whisked into the hospital's Cardiac Care Unit and hooked up to various monitoring devices, which diagnosed a rapidly progressing, left ventricular myocardiac infarction, a common kind of heart attack.

The staff administered the standard intervention, but it failed. Starved of oxygenated blood, a large portion of the muscular left walls of Earl's heart died.

By feeding an array of drugs into his bloodstream, the doctors brought Earl to a momentarily stable condition and eventually they sent him home. A few weeks later, though, he was rushed back to the hospital. This pattern held through the summer, fall and early winter. Earl would spend a week or two in hospital on the verge of death—from cardiac arrhythmias, heart arrest, congestive heart failure, intramural thrombus (an aneurysm formed in the left wall of his heart), but mainly fulminant pneumonia and kidney failure— because his heart had become an inadequate pump. Again and again, the cardiac unit staff brought him back, with oxygen therapy or a pacemaker or drugs that lessen, in various ways, the work that the heart has to do. Again and again, Earl rallied, and his doctors sent him home with a virtual pharmacopoeia—Digoxin, Capoten,

Lasix, Quinaglute, Zaroxolyn, Coumadin, Potassium chloride, sublingual nitroglycerine. At home in Northampton, Jean ministered to him. Visiting nurses helped out. For a while he'd seem to improve, but it was never more than a few weeks before he was being driven back to the hospital, gasping for air.

Only a decade or so before, Earl would probably have died shortly after his heart attack. The steady advance of cardiac pharmacology deserved much of the credit, perhaps also the blame, for his having survived these last six months. But even some medical people, whose professional training should have cured them of metaphysical thoughts, expressed surprise at Earl's durability.

After Earl's most recent and most serious bout with the complications of living with a half-dead heart, his family doctor recommended that he go to a nursing home, at least for a while. The doctor felt Earl needed twenty-four-hour care of a sort that would bc hard to arrange at home.

For Earl, entering Linda Manor was nightmarish. He didn't mind the routine full-body check that the nurses performed the day he arrived or the crinkly feel of the plastic bedcover under his sheets. He was used to hospital beds and procedures. In fact, he wished Linda Manor felt more like a hospital and less like a place designed for long stays. What frightened him most was the line-up of residents across the nurses' station, old men and women sitting there with their mouths open and heads lolling to one side. They clearly had arrived at the end of the line. He didn't belong here among them, did he?

A few days after Earl arrived one of the evening nurses wrote in his chart:

> Disturbed that wife couldn't come in this p.m. Has called
> her 4 times begging to be removed from here, says he
> feels 'trapped'.

Earl hadn't ordered his own phone. He didn't plan to stay long enough to justify the expense. His first days he made so many trips, padding along behind his wheelchair, half out of breath, down the long central corridor to the public pay phone, that for a time the staff thought he must be demented. He was not. Earl was calling almost everyone he knew, just to hear familiar voices.

Earl felt so desperate to call yet another old friend and tell him where he was that sometimes he'd push his wheelchair out to the nurses' station and beg permission to use the phone there. He had to wait, surrounded by distressing sights and sounds. And there was always that line-up along the wall. One ninety year-old man sat by the water fountain, calling out while stamping his feet: 'Seventy-seven turkeys. May his soul rest in peace. God save the King. Seventy-one-five. Please Lord, let the country prosper. Amen.' Deep in reverie, he believed himself to be simultaneously at a turkey-shoot and playing a church organ. A woman, who always wore a turban, sat at the other end of the line-up, issuing orders to passers-by. She believed this was a hotel and that she owned it. Often she sat there conversing with the parakeet in the cage to her left. The bird inside could speak the woman's name and would now and then utter a long and drawn out 'Yee-ahsss' in an accent just like hers. A man without any legs sat nearby, calling out, 'He'p me! He'p me out! Wanna go back to bed!' When Earl first heard that man's voice, it went right through him.

About a week after his arrival at Linda Manor, Earl's family doctor visited him in his room. Jean waited outside in the corridor. Earl thought he was prepared for the worst, although he hoped, of course, for good news.

'Listen, Doc, I'm not a kid any more. I want to know where I stand.'

Earl's family doctor had heard this question many times. He was in his sixties and had made a speciality of geriatric medicine. He liked dealing with elderly patients in part because they usually permitted him to be candid. As Earl had told him several times that he worried about Jean managing her own financial affairs without him—Jean had lost her first husband in a car accident and for a long time afterwards had found herself utterly lost among bills and cheque-books—the family doctor thought he owed Earl an honest answer. He wasn't God, he said, but he doubted that Earl would be alive in six months. And, he added, a fatal event could occur suddenly, at any time.

How soon at the earliest? Earl wanted to know.

The doctor didn't want to say.

Earl pressed him for an answer. 'I'm not a kid any more.'

Finally, the doctor gave in. Maybe a week, he said.

Some months later, recalling the day when he delivered that bad news, Earl's doctor remarked, 'People usually want to know. They don't usually want to hear it.'

Sunlight stretched across the grey linoleum floor of Earl's room. Earl lay on his bedspread, in clothes he could have played golf in, except for the slippers he wore and the oxygen catheter. His slippers were made of brown leather, appropriate to a banker in his boudoir. Jean sat beside him, a handsome, stocky woman in her sixties, with broad red cheeks, dressed in tweeds. Earl's clothes hung loosely around him. But his voice had a quick, birdlike energy. 'If I'm gonna die, I want to die at home or in a hospital. Not here.'

Jean rose from her chair and straightened the collar of Earl's turtle-neck. He submitted without protest as she smoothed down his grey hair, which had been sticking up in back. 'Like a rooster's,' she said.

'I don't want to kick the bucket here,' Earl went on, looking up at her.

'But you're a tough old cookie.'

'I've escaped five other times.' Earl gazed at the wall across from his bed.

'It's a dirty trick.'

'Boy, it is. Here I was, seventy-eight and feeling like a fifty-year-old.'

'And then, kafooey, you lose all this stuff overnight practically. You think if you live a good life, keep active and healthy . . .'

Earl smiled. 'We travelled all over the place.'

She smiled back. 'But you're a spark-plug. I have plenty of good ideas, but you *move* on them. We did more stuff because of that.'

'I'd like to get home.' Earl looked away, then back at her, and the matter-of-fact, manly quality he then put in his voice did not entirely conceal the plaintiveness, as he said, 'I hope it's gonna be this weekend.'

'Well, don't push it, honey.' Jean looked down at her lap. 'Please don't push it. I'd like to have just a calm weekend, before you come home.'

'Well, OK,' Earl said briskly. His voice quickened. 'Then let's make it Monday. If it'll help you.'

'That would be much better.'

Earl's room-mate often sat on the other side of the room in his wheelchair facing the television, which belonged to him. He didn't seem to listen in on Jean and Earl's conversation, but now and then he broke into it. He seemed to be talking to them. 'Those boys they put in the CC camps during the Depression got thirty a month and we got fifteen. That caused a lot of resentment,' he said. 'And there was this coloured girl had a baby right on the trail.'

'Goodness,' Jean said. She turned back to Earl.

'Those garbage disposal units, they all have a reset on them,' Earl's room-mate said.

'You want your TV on?' Earl called from his bed.

'I don't care,' said his room-mate from his wheelchair.

Earl picked up the television remote control. His room-mate sometimes had trouble operating the thing. Earl flicked on the television. 'He likes soap operas,' Earl explained to Jean as voices full of intrigue and passion, from *Days of Our Lives*, filled the room.

The television seemed a comforting presence at this moment. It erected a barrier around Jean and Earl in their corner of the room. They talked for a while about the trip to Florida that they had planned for March. 'I was hoping we'd go, but it doesn't look like it,' Earl said. 'I just want to get home. The doctor gave me a week to six months.'

'But you mustn't think of that as a sentence,' Jean said. 'That's just a guess. I wish he hadn't said anything.'

'I did say, "Now, lookit, Doctor. I'm not a kid any more." And he said, "A week or six months."' Earl looked pensive. He pursed his lips. 'If I'm gonna go, I'd just as soon go fast and not suffer through another heart attack.' Then he looked at Jean again, as if trying to read her face, and said, 'But I want to die at home.'

'But we have a friend who was given four months and lived

seven years,' Jean said.

'The point is, the atmosphere here isn't helping.'

'I don't think it's the atmosphere.' Jean leaned close to him. She touched his leg. 'It's what's happening to you. You have a nice room and services at your fingertips that you wouldn't have at home. You've got to be creative about it.'

They talked about Earl's children for a while, and which one would take his death hardest. Earl then had to ask Jean to excuse him for a moment, which was code between them for the fact that he needed to use the urinal bottle. Diuretics, to lessen his heart's labour and prevent congestive heart failure, had long since become a fact of his life.

Jean went out. She stood at the glassed-in, west-facing end of the corridor, gazing out at the parking lot. The landscape was sunny and icy-looking. She looked tired. Her phone had rung at seven o'clock this morning, and her heart pounded as she picked it up. But it was someone from the security service saying there'd been a burglary in the neighbourhood last night.

For six months she'd lived with her nerves on edge. Five times Jean had driven Earl to the hospital, left him there and come home to her large empty house, wondering whether this time she should prepare for a funeral or another less than joyous homecoming. Several times the doctors predicted that Earl wouldn't rally, and the whole family gathered. Jean couldn't remember how many nights she'd spent on couches in the hospital's waiting-rooms, sometimes sneaking past the nurses into Earl's room for a late-night chat. For months she'd had her house invaded by medical strangers and medical equipment. A compulsion for privacy was a weakness of hers, she knew. 'I'm a picture-straightener.'

She didn't know whether she had the strength to take Earl home again. She gazed out at the frozen landscape, the sun so bright on the icy grass it made her squint. Her first husband had died in the early spring, many years ago. He had died suddenly, in a car accident. Memories of the aftermath were fresh again.

Jean had found advantages in a second marriage in the years after children. One came to such a marriage fully formed. Of course, Earl had a lot to do with that. He let her feel that way. They had an almost perfect partnership. She tended to get fuddled over little things, like balancing a cheque-book. A routine notice from the IRS could upset her greatly. She'd worry aloud, and Earl would say, 'Don't worry. It'll be all right.' And it always was all right. Confronted with a problem he couldn't solve himself, Earl had only to pick up the phone to make everything all right again. He had strength and boundless energy. Those qualities, Jean thought, were very attractive to a woman, to this woman especially. She felt very safe with him.

Jean understood why Earl wanted to come home to die. But she meant more than she'd said back in the room, when she'd told him that she didn't want him dying at home. She didn't want to feel complicitous in his death, and she felt all worn out with anguish and the effort, more mental than physical, of keeping him alive. While Earl was here at Linda Manor, others had that responsibility. Standing at the windows at the corridor's end, Jean rubbed her hands, as if to warm them against the chill on the other side of the glass. Behind her and in front of her she saw months of wakeful nights. She couldn't bring Earl home yet.

Earl sat on the edge of his bed. Holding his shoulders erect, he gingerly picked up the silvery, helmet-like cover from his lunch. He stared at the plate of stir-fry. "I don't know what it is,' he said. He stared down at it. 'That's enough to make me *not* eat.' He picked up the fork and paused again. He had to eat or he'd have no chance of beating the doctor's prediction, or at least of getting well enough to go home. He scooped up a small bite and quickly slipped it into his mouth. The food had no taste. But he ate on.

He couldn't go home this week, not in this condition. In fact, he couldn't even make the trip to the dining-room. His doctor thought it best that Earl eat in his room. He didn't mind. In the dining-room, he'd shared his table with a hearty fellow who told him that he himself had trouble eating when he first came here, but that Earl's lack of appetite would surely pass. But there was also a woman at their table who had seemed perfectly rational until he saw her trying to eat her soup with a fork. She began complaining that her utensil didn't work. Another time she mixed her ice-cream with her mashed potatoes. Earl missed the company, but not the dining-room. He just wished that he had an appetite and that his diarrhoea would go away.

Earl got the last wish. The next morning, when the charge nurse Mary Ann came in with his pills, Earl grimaced and said to her, 'Now I have the opposite problem.' Mary Ann, buxom and jolly, was Earl's favourite nurse. She was one of those who believed that older, simpler forms of medicine should supersede drugs. She sat down on the bed beside Earl and put her arm around his shoulder, chatting about nothing of consequence until he seemed somewhat cheered up.

The next day, his diarrhoea returned. Earl lay on his bedspread after another attack. 'Sometimes I don't want to live,' Earl said. 'I *want* to live. But not in this condition. I was involved in every civic activity known to man.' He shook his head.

In fact, it didn't take much to make Earl happy. Among some of the staff, however, he had begun to acquire a reputation for being troublesome. 'Demanding' was the word of choice for residents like Earl, and the word sometimes acquired a cold significance. Earl had now been here for nearly three weeks, and nurses' entries full of irritation had begun appearing in his chart:

> Very demanding of staff—ordering them to do things for him that he is able to do for himself, i.e. change TV control buttons.

Many residents presented special difficulties, especially to the nurses' aides, who in any nursing home stand near the bottom of the pay scale and do the most arduous work. The aides cleaned and dressed and often fed the residents. They lifted and transported them. Often they received harsh words or worse for their pains.

The problem wasn't that the work revolted the nurses' aides. Those who couldn't stand the smell of other people's excrement rarely made it through their probationary period. The work was simply hard, and harder now since the staff cuts. These had begun after New Year's and, to none of the aides' surprise, had fallen heaviest on them. 'That's the way it always is. No one ever takes people off the top, just off the bottom,' one remarked. The cuts meant that every aide had at least one more resident, and often two more, on her list, and the difference was profound. For most aides, the cuts meant they had less time to spend consoling residents and listening to their life stories. For a few, the cuts just meant more work, and more work left undone. One day around this time, the daughter of a resident found that her father had been lying in his own excrement for about two hours. That was not supposed to happen at Linda Manor. The administrator was furious. Nothing excused such negligence. Eventually an aide was fired. Morale had never sunk so low. Earl had arrived at the wrong time.

The last thing the staff needed was another demanding resident. When a resident rang the call-bell, a beeper went off at the nurses' station and a white light went on above the resident's door. To the aides, it seemed as if every time they looked, Earl's light was on. Sometimes it was Earl's room-mate who pressed the call bell. Sometimes Earl pressed it on his room-mate's behalf. But even then, it seemed, Earl had something he wanted done for himself as well. What did he think this was? And Earl seemed upset when the staff didn't answer his bell right away. The policy was that they should answer the routine bells within fifteen minutes. That was the best they could do. Earl ought to understand that.

But to Earl, fifteen minutes could feel like an eternity. He kept his alarm near at hand—a small capsule with a nipple-like red button on the end, attached to a white electrical cord that snaked out from the wall. This was Earl's umbilical cord now, but it didn't make him feel safe. 'They come when they get a *chance*,' Earl fretted.

The last few nights a certain aide had made night-time almost unendurable. Whenever she came in, she looked cross and seemed impatient. Earl had been trying to think of a way to let her know who he was. No one around here seemed to know who he was. This aide didn't seem to think he was even human. But the thought of offending her, and the possible consequences, chilled Earl. He'd held his tongue and endured her coldness.

The windows across the room were black. His diarrhoea had abated, but Earl wanted to wear a diaper just in case. The aide answered the call-bell after a while, that same cold, unfriendly aide. He made his request. She said, 'No, you cannot have one.' No explanation, just that curt answer.

Confrontation had never been Earl's style. He thought he ought to speak up, but he was frightened. And yet he felt he couldn't endure this, being denied a simple disposable brief. Should he or shouldn't he? He took a quick breath, and said, 'You know, young lady, you don't like me very much.'

The aide seemed surprised. 'Why do you say that?'

Earl felt safer now. 'Well, you come in here, you never wear a smile. It's almost as if you're doing me a favour.'

Earl told Jean the whole story the next morning. 'She took it pretty well. She said she was sorry she was acting that way. She didn't realize it. I was afraid to do it, but I figured I'd better take the bull by the horns.'

'That's good,' Jean said. 'Because, you know, you sometimes have a grouchy expression, and people don't know how sweet you are inside.' She sat in the armchair beside his bed. Earl sat on his bedspread, sitting upright against the pillows, fully dressed as usual, as if he were merely resting for a moment here.

Domestic routines survive even in foxholes. Jean had brought in Earl's laundry. Now she put it away for him in his photo-wood-grain-finished Linda Manor bureau, took off her coat and, leaning down, gave him his morning kiss. She offered him her hands, to feel the coldness of the air outside, and did up a couple of the shirt buttons that Earl had missed.

'What did you have for lunch yesterday?' he asked.

'Veal, which you know I love. And we sat near a sunny window . . . ' Jean went on a while.

'A long lunch,' said Earl, dreamy and smiling. 'But when the girls get together, it takes a long time.'

These morning on the way to the nursing home, Jean always stopped at a favourite diner for breakfast.

'Tomorrow,' Earl said now, 'when you leave the diner, get the paper automatically.' That was his way of reproving her for not having brought today's paper.

'I would have,' she said. 'But it was so cold. My hand would have frozen to the machine.'

'We can't have that.'

'Besides, you just throw it away,' she said.

'I scan it,' Earl said.

'Whatever you say, dear. You're the boss.'

'I love that statement.'

'Enjoy it while you can.'

This was what a wife would say to a husband on the mend. Earl beamed. The morning sunlight stretched across the light grey linoleum floor, improving it. Earl and Jean might have been just another well-matched couple, savouring the start of another day together. Musingly, Earl said he thought he'd go to hear Lou's daughter read at Literary Hour next Tuesday. Then he turned to Jean, his eyes searching her face, and said, 'If I'm not home by then.'

Jean looked away towards the bright window.

'Hear that, dear?' Earl said.

'Well, I don't know.' She smiled a little. 'I heard you.' She looked at him and placed her hand on his leg. 'I have to go to the dentist Tuesday. So you just have to take it easy.'

'OK,' Earl said, 'Wednesday.'

Jean didn't answer and soon changed the subject. Jean couldn't say, yes, she'd take him home next Wednesday, because she believed in keeping promises. But she didn't believe in telling him everything that was on her mind. She often visited Earl three times a day and stayed for several hours each time. After her last visit, she'd go out to her car in the dark. She would not let herself begin to cry until she was safely inside the car, but she cried all the way home to her empty house.

Earl died in his room the following morning. Across from the nurses' station sat the usual line-up of residents in wheelchairs—the woman in the turban, the man playing the organ and competing in a turkey shoot, the others who sat and seemed to gaze at nothing, and a very old woman who sometimes declaimed prayers aloud. She was chanting, eerily, 'The Lord Jesus Christ. We may die according to the flesh and live . . . ' No one had told her that someone had died, but she clearly sensed something amiss. Her voice trailed off into incoherent mutterings and rose again, as she cried to her God, 'Help! Me! Help! Me!' Earl's room-mate sat across the way, in his wheelchair in front of the nurses' station counter. He was weeping. Several aides and nurses hovered around him. 'At least he didn't suffer,' said Earl's room-mate, through his sobs. Behind the counter a nurse stood holding the telephone, saying to someone in the kitchen, 'I want to let you know that Earl Duncan has died. Just so you won't send us a tray for him.' It was the sort of scene Earl would have hated, the sort that had intensified his hopes of escape.

Alone in her house last night, Jean awakened nearly every hour, carrying up with her into consciousness, like a vivid dream, the thought that Earl was in trouble. When she got the call this morning, Jean felt stunned, but not surprised.

Driving out on Route 9 towards Linda Manor, Jean wondered if she could have done something to prevent his dying. She wondered why, after knowing for so long that this was bound to happen soon, she still could not believe that it had.

A veteran nurse-administrator whom Jean scarcely knew hugged her, then led her to the room. Jean sat in the armchair beside Earl's bed. He looked like himself, but waxen. Jean sat and stroked his arm. Now and then she patted the sheet that covered his leg. 'I never take steps now without a lot of emotion, which is hard for an old WASP,' she said. She cried without sound, just a steady mist of tears. 'He's the most social animal I have ever known. I got jealous of his time sometimes, because I wanted more of him. He's a dear man, a very spiritual man, but not holier-than-thou. He loved going to church and he worked for the Church. I don't know what he thinks of the life to come, but he lived this life wonderfully, every minute. He was totally comfortable in the world.'

Jean stood up, leaned over and kissed his cheek. She picked up her pocketbook and left. She got all the way to her car and then decided to return. 'I just like to be with him,' she told Susan, the social worker, who stopped in at the room for a little while. Jean wanted to avoid the telephone for a while, too. It is customary to think of friends and relatives as props to the bereaved. The reality of widowhood, as Jean well knew, is that the widow also ends up propping up the friends and relatives and playing hostess to them. She needed some time before she made the necessary calls.

Sitting there, stroking Earl's arm, Jean suddenly thought she felt him move. She shook herself. 'I just can't believe he isn't going to wake up.'

Deaths in-house were first announced on the erasable bulletin board inside the kitchen, out of the view of residents. The name would be printed in magic marker followed by 'Deceased'. The 'In Loving Memory' form would be posted within a day or two, on the obituary board in the main corridor. Sue, the activities director, or her aide usually wrote the brief encomiums. These usually included a standard line or two—'A loving woman,' 'Will be missed by family, friends and staff.' Sue and her assistant strove to convey something of the person's individuality, but there wasn't always much to say—'A lover of plants,' 'An avid bingo player,' 'Enjoyed children.' In many cases, the deceased had been essentially anonymous. Earl's memorial was of a piece: 'A kind and gracious gentleman, who loved his family, friends and the sport of golfing.'

The residents who came to the monthly memorial services, held before bingo in the activity room, sometimes knew much more. Winifred, who always attended, would have a lot to say about many of the people who died that month. But even she would come up short on one or two. 'I don't recall ever seeing him,' she'd said of one of the dead who had been honoured at last month's service. 'But I miss knowing that he's not with us any more.'

The morning of Earl's death, several female residents sat in the activity room, sipping coffee and munching doughnuts, a downstairs late-morning coffee klatch. 'Too bad,' said one. 'But it's a good thing. He had cancer.' No one had really known him.

Lou had never gotten to know Earl well. Joe wasn't sure he'd ever spoken to Earl. Joe read the notice on the bulletin board. Up in the room, Joe said of Earl, 'He was seventy-nine. If I had a heart attack at seventy-nine, I'd say all right. I feel bad about him, but Jesus Christ his age and all.'

'Let's think of something else,' said Lou.

Hospice

Lou had something else on his mind. He sat down by the window and gave Joe his usual summary of Current Events and then, shifting in his chair, lifting a hand, index finger extended, Lou said, 'Changing the subject a little. Talking about tools.'

Joe grinned. He sat up in his bed and, still grinning, said, 'I wasn't aware we were talking about tools.' Joe lay back and, with a visible effort, stifled his laughter.

'I was up last night trying to figure this out,' Lou said. 'Millers Falls. They made tools somewhere around here. Are they still in business?' Lou didn't wait for an answer. He lifted an index finger again. 'The first tool I ever bought myself was a hand-drill. I was working in a shop that made electrical fixtures. I had to drill small holes. And I paid three dollars and fifty cents for that drill, and three dollars and fifty cents was my wages for the week, and that tool is still in good working order. I gave it to my grandson. It has the Millers Falls label on the handle.'

Still grinning, Joe sat up again and said towards Lou, 'Changing the subject a little.'

'A hundred and ninety degrees.' Lou smiled. 'Go ahead, Joe.'

'I don't have anything to say.' Joe lay back and let his laughter out. Then, the trace of a smile on his face, Joe lay listening to Lou reminisce.

The first tool, the seventy-eight-year-old Millers Falls hand-drill, was like fertilizing an egg in Lou's memory. That tool seemed to carry all the information Lou needed to reconstitute his long life. The tool could lead backwards: Lou finishing eighth grade on a Thursday in 1914 and skipping the graduation ceremony in order to start his first full-time job. Turning over his three-dollars-fifty pay cheque to his mother who somehow managed always to put food on the table for a large family. His father's delivery service that ended in failure when his horse went lame. Shutting his eyes tight, Lou described Philadelphia and repopulated it, with that Irish cop with a voice like Joe's and that hawker down in the Tenderloin.

That old hand-drill took Lou through his long succession of jobs, helping to wire up factories and shipyards. With that hand-drill and a can of shoe polish, for covering up scratches in baseboards, Lou once again brought electricity to the houses of Philadelphia.

There was something beautiful about Lou in the act of story-telling, opening up this storehouse of memories and bringing them back to life. He summoned up his memories with what seemed like the force of necessity. Telling his stories, he sat still in his chair, but his hands became animated. If he was interrupted mid-course, by a visit from an aide or a nurse, he would stop. He might even chat with the intruder, but his fingers would stroke the arms of his chair or drum lightly upon them, and when the intruder departed, he would pick up his story just where he'd left off.

Joe had heard a joke about two prisoners locked up together so long that they no longer tell each other their jokes. One simply says, 'Thirty-six,' and the other at once begins laughing hysterically. Maybe he and Lou—retelling the same stories over and over again—would one day resemble those prisoners: two old pensioners who had run out of new things to say to each other. Local news was scant; around here a new story usually had to do with someone's new ailment. Lou's old stories were much more entertaining. Heard only twice, Lou's memories could seem monotonous. Heard many times, they were like old friends. They were comforting. Lou's memories seemed like an immortal part of him. They existed right now forever. Lou's memories contained such a density of life that in their presence death seemed impossible.

Lou was on a roll now, once again. 'In Philadelphia, shortly after I married, my brother bought a Ford. There was no stick shift in those days.'

'Well, they hadda crank it up first,' Joe said.

'That's not the main part of the story.'

Joe, looking at the ceiling, closed his lips in an exaggerated way and smiled.

Lou went on. 'And they didn't have traffic lights at the crossings. The cops stood in intersections with signs.' Lou shifted in his chair. 'Anyhow, this Sunday morning my brother called me up. He said, "There isn't much traffic, I'll take you out and teach you how to drive." Out on Broad and Fairmount, he put me in the driver's side. I couldn't see any traffic. I was tense as hell. But we were riding along pretty good.'

Joe chuckled at what was coming.

'Anyhow,' Lou said. 'We got out to Twenty-Second. I don't know what happened. I lost control and drove up on the pavement. And where do we go but right beside the prison gate. Fortunately, we didn't hit it, and my brother says, 'Let's get the hell out of here before someone sees us.' And that's how I didn't learn to drive. That's my one and only time behind the wheel of a car.'

Lou went on for a while. Then he returned to the present. 'Hey, Joe, incidentally, what's the definition of "hospice"?'

Joe shook his head. Lou was amazing. Sometimes Lou would get to thinking about his wife and say, 'I think I've seen about everything God meant me to see.' And then, often moments later, he'd raise his index finger and say, 'Incidentally, Joe . . . ' He'd want to know if Joe knew what this term they kept using on the radio, 'Dolby sound,' meant. If humanity continued to extract such vast amounts of minerals, oil and water from the earth, would the globe collapse? Did chickens raised in incubators lose their nesting instinct? Could hail be used as ice-cubes if it was tainted with acid rain? Could you eat salmon after they'd spawned? If vultures ate tainted meat, why didn't they get sick? 'Sitting here, I think of some of the damnedest things,' Lou said once. He didn't have to tell Joe that. Lou would sit in his chair, his brow knitted, his lips pursed, like a student at an arithmetic problem, and Joe would know that pretty soon a question would be asked. What was chicory? Someone had said a wild duck had been seen on the grounds outside. What did a wild duck look like? What was the origin of the expression, 'freeze the balls off a brass monkey?' Did anyone ever try filling a football with helium? If someone down on the first floor and someone up on the second each simultaneously pushed the button to summon the same elevator, what would happen? Where did the expression, 'sow your wild oats' come from? What kind of wood were George Washington's teeth made from? They'd been discussing that one for three months.

When Joe didn't know the answer, which was usually, Lou would hold the question until Ruth came in. The other day Lou asked Ruth, in a very puzzled voice, 'I wonder what lesbians actually do?' Then with sudden force, Lou said to his sixty-five-year-old daughter, 'But don't *you* tell me.'

Ruth told Joe that it had gotten to the point where her friend the reference librarian wouldn't even say hello to her. The librarian would see Ruth coming and say, 'All right, what does your father want to know now?' The man was almost ninety-two years old, and he asked more questions than any child Joe had known. Joe used to think seventy-two was old. Well, it still was, as far as Joe was concerned. Life was mysterious. Maybe ninety-one was, in its way, younger.

What was the definition of 'hospice'? Lou had asked a moment ago.

Joe looked thoughtful. 'I don't know,' Joe said finally.

Then, suddenly, Joe sat up. 'Here. I'll go get the, uh, medical thing. They got a, a . . . Oh, what the hell.'

Joe's steel brace clattered on the floor. He was putting on his orthopaedic shoes.

'Where ya goin'?' Lou asked.

'Well, I'm gonna find out what "hospice" means. They got a, uh, medical dictionary.'

Lou rolled his shoulders and settled back in his chair, his eyes shut, like an old cat in the sun.

Joe headed out towards the nurses' station. He limped along on his cane down the carpeted hallway, then stopped for a moment to rest and catch his breath. 'Lou's always thinking of these things. It's good. It keeps him active.'

Joe started on again, limping towards the nurses' station and the medical dictionary. 'Keeps *me* active.'

GRANTA

MARY KARR
GRANDMA MOORE'S CANCER

Maybe it's wrong to blame the arrival of Grandma Moore for much of the worst hurt in my family, but I do. Before, our lives had been closed to outsiders. The noise of my parents' fights might leak out through the screens at night, and I might guess at the neighbours' scorn, but nobody inquired about our Trouble, about Mother's being Nervous. We didn't go to church. No one came to visit. We probably seemed as blurry to the rest of the neighbourhood as bad television. Suddenly Grandma was staring at us with laser-blue eyes from behind horn-rims, saying *Can I make a suggestion?* or beginning every sentence with *Why don't you . . . ?* She bustled around as if she had some earnest agenda, but God knows what it was. She carried an enormous black alligator doctor's bag, which held, along with the regular lady stuff in there—cosmetics and little peony-embroidered hankies—the kind of honest-to-God hacksaw used by criminals in B-movies to saw through jail bars. My sister Lecia and I had a standing joke that we were keeping Grandma prisoner, and she was planning to bust out.

I had always thought what I lacked in my family was some attentive, brownie-baking female to keep my hair curled and generally Donna-Reed over me. But my behaviour got worse with Grandma's new order. I became a nail-biter. My tantrums escalated to the point where even Daddy didn't think they were funny. I tore down the new drapes they'd hung at the dining-room windows and clawed scratch marks down both of Lecia's cheeks. Beating me didn't work. Though I was a world-famous crybaby, I refused to cry during spankings. I still can recall Daddy holding his belt, my calves striped with its imprint and stinging and me saying, 'Go on and hit me then, if it makes you feel like a man to beat on a little girl like me.' End of spanking.

In fairness to Grandma, she was dying of cancer at fifty, which can't do much for your disposition. Still, I remember not one tender feeling for or from her. Her cheek was withered like a bad apple and smelled of hyacinth. I had to be physically forced to kiss this cheek, even though I was prone to throwing my arms around the neck of any vaguely friendly grown-up—vacuum-cleaner salesmen, mechanics, checkout ladies.

Opposite: Grandma Moore with Mary Karr's mother, 1923.

I had this succinct way of explaining the progression of my Grandmother's cancer to neighbour ladies who asked: 'First, they took off her toenail, then her toe, then her foot. Then they shot mustard gas through her leg till it was burnt black, and she screamed for six weeks non-stop. Then they took off her leg, and it was like a black stump laid up on a pillow. When we went to see her, she called Lecia by the wrong name. Then she came home, and it went to her brain, so she went crazy, and ants were crawling all over her arm. Then she died.'

At the end of this report, Lecia and I would start scanning around whoever's kitchen it was for cookies or Kool-Aid. We knew with certain instinct that reporting on a dead grandma deserved some payoff. After a while, Lecia even mustered some tears, which could jack up the ante as high as a Popsicle. I couldn't have cried for Grandma under torture, but I knew my spiel and I blindly counted on people's pity to get me what I wanted.

For a long time Grandma's slow death from cancer stayed fenced inside that pat report. Perhaps the neighbour ladies who heard me tell it were justly horrified by my lack of grief instead of being wowed—as I intended them to be—by how well I was bearing up. I fooled no one worse than I fooled myself by blotting out the whole eighteen-month horror show.

At first if I try to conjure up that period, some general ideas trickle back, but no specific events. I remember, for example, that Lecia kowtowed to the old lady because it kept the peace and bought her points with Mother. I just tried to slip around her, the reasons for which are vague—maybe she liked to wash me or to pull at my hair snarls with a fine-toothed comb—but the central feeling that arises from memory of that time is a kind of fear that starts at the base of my spine and creeps upward till it borders on low-level panic. Even now, part of me flinches at any mention of her. I would just as soon keep that wheelchair she occupied in my head empty of its ghost.

Maybe this aversion comes from a kid's intolerance for the infirm. Truly I could not gin up much enthusiasm for them. Maybe some kids can: maybe there are Christian children reared with deep saintly streaks who read scripture to their rotting grandparents in the early dusk. I did not. Grandma lasted too long and made my mother cry too much.

Besides, we hadn't known her that well before she got sick. I had inherited her name, Mary, but she had been little more than that name carefully executed in Venus pencil on a series of construction-paper cards. One of these was red and heart-shaped, pasted on to a lacy paper doily. It got saved in Daddy's gold cigar-box, for some reason. The envelope has M. D. Anderson Hospital (which is now the Houston Medical Center) for an address. The heart opens up to this odd message: 'Dear Grandma, I hope you are getting better. There was a man in a car wreck who died three feet tall. Here is the man.' Then there's a horizontal stick figure with X's for eyes next to a bubble-shaped car with what looks like a Band-aid on it. I guess that was my studied approximation of death, at the time.

Still, no matter how blank a gaze you try to put on remembering an ugly illness to protect yourself from the sheer tedium of it, if you spend any time at all speaking about it to some nodding psychiatrist you will eventually stumble into a deep silence. And from that silence in your skull there will develop— almost chemically, like film paper doused in that magic solution— a snapshot of cold horror. It's not the old man you glimpsed with arthritic fingers trying to open one of those little black, click-open purses for soda change at the Coke machine. It isn't even the toddler you once passed in a yard behind a chain-link fence tethered to a clothesline like a dog in midday heat. Those are only rumours of suffering. Real suffering has a face and a smell. And it knows your name.

The doctors piped mustard gas through Grandma's leg to try to stop the spread of her melanoma. When I grew up and read about the Great War, how clouds of mustard gas floated over trenches and seared the lungs of soldiers, I couldn't begin to fathom the doctors' reasoning in applying it to that old woman, whose fair-complexioned leg was charred by the treatment into something petrified-looking. She did, according to my mother, scream without break for weeks, not days, this despite morphine. Then gangrene set in, and they had to amputate anyway.

The idea of Grandma losing her leg didn't bother me much at first because it seemed in the realm of make-believe. Lecia and I fancied her having a wheelchair we could take for rides. Also, this was about the time Peter Pan was big, so I tended to imagine her with a peg-leg, like a pirate. Riding in the car to the hospital that first day, I even drew a picture of her with a wooden peg and a plumed hat with skull and crossbones. Lecia had the infinite good sense to fold this into quarters and rathole it in her back pocket before Mother got a glimpse of it.

But Mother was running on such psychic overdrive that it might not have even registered. As Nervous as she tended to be, she could always rally in times of crisis. Really, she was something to watch. I have seen her dismantle and reassemble a washing machine, stitch up a dress from a thirty-piece *Vogue* pattern in a day, ace a college calculus course when she went back to school at forty and lay brick. We used to say that if she really had her titty in a wringer, she would flat go to work wrestling it out. Grandma's sickness was such a time. All trace of Nervous just evaporated from my mother. Her chin tilted up to suggest a kind of determined ease.

There must have been rules back then about kids not being on cancer wards. But Mother had the idea that we would cheer Grandma up. Plus Daddy was working days, and she had run out of people to leave us with. I'd never been in a hospital before. And of course what you generally remember from that era is the smell of Pine Sol—and all the impressive running around, people being wheeled in and out with tubes and bottles swaying over them.

My memory of the hospital gets vivid at the instant when Lecia pulled my elbow to turn me away from a guy horking up what looked like clean water into a little kidney-shaped silver pan. I turned from the sick man and entered the invisible cloud of odours that floated around Mother at that time: Shalimar perfume and tobacco and peppermint Lifesavers. She had on a long army-green silk dress and a brown alligator belt from Chanel. Her high heels hardly made any noise the way she set her foot down in them. She had a long stride and led with her thigh like a fashion model. Her hair was short and thick and brushed straight back from her face and looked from my height like a lion's mane.

She pushed open some double doors. You could hear somebody crying *Please please please* but in a whispery voice. We passed the room of a surprisingly young woman whose black hair was woven into a big tower. She lay back on a La-Z-Boy recliner holding a red rubber enema bottle pressed against her jaw, and you could hear organ music from a radio ballgame. Then we were at Grandma's room, easing a big silent door open.

The really shocking thing about an amputation is how crude it looks. You would think that they could tidy it up; maybe now they do. Anybody who has ever had to dismantle a deer with a hunting knife or even fry up a chicken or rabbit knows how brutal it feels to hack through bone and cartilage, but I had expected Grandma's lopped-off leg to seem more like a doll's, bloodless and neat. Maybe I expected a bandage on it.

They had taken the leg off above the knee, and Grandma's thigh was propped on a hospital pillow. There were still streaks of black running from the stump-end in narrowing rivers. Whether these were from the gas burns or the subsequent blood poisoning, I don't know. You could see how they'd tried to save enough flesh from the thigh to fold it over the cut bone. Somebody had tried to stitch it all down neatly so it might look as if it had grown that way, but you could tell from the stitching that the edges were randomly folded over in the ragged way you might try to close up a pork roast you were stuffing. The stitches were flat black and pinched at her very white skin. Plus they had slathered some kind of ointment all over the thigh, so the whole thing looked painfully shiny and wet. Even with the five bunches of flowers her sisters had sent, the room reeked of something like a stinging horse liniment I had smelled on a ranch once.

I wanted to leave right away just looking at that leg, but the door had hissed shut behind us, and Grandma's face was rolling towards us already. She was so thin and pale you could practically see straight through her. Her lips were bluish and her hair had got whiter, so that her eyes, when the lids flickered open, seemed a strong shade, but were at the same time bleached out, as if she'd seen something that had scalded her inside. Lecia walked right over to the edge of the bed like it was no big deal. Grandma opened and closed her mouth a few times like a fish, not saying anything. They had taken out her dentures, which sat on a napkin on top of her bed table. There were also those little white strings of spit running between her lips, and she had some yellow crust in the corners. Mother said that somebody really might have washed her up and put her teeth in, but she didn't seem alarmed really. That put me off, because I could usually count on Mother to be at least as big a sissy as me; I was ready to bolt. Grandma's hand patted the mattress by her, and Lecia grabbed it. That made Grandma suck in her breath suddenly, so Lecia dropped the hand and took a pace back. Then Mother stepped in and smoothed Grandma's white hair back gently and asked how she felt. Grandma just started patting the bed again. She fixed that empty stare on Lecia as if she had just descended to the bedside from the clouds. She sucked in her breath hard and said, 'Belinda! Where have you been? Thank God, Belinda.' Then her voice got quiet again, and she went on and on about how she'd missed her and looked for her, and Lecia just played along like she was this person we'd never heard of.

Before we left, Mother threw a screaming cuss fit at the two doctors who'd done the mustard gas treatment. It was never fun when Mother raised hell in public but in this instance I almost welcomed it. After being shut down all day, zombie-like, she seemed to descend back into her body. The doctors just stood with their coffee mugs, as if it didn't occur to them to walk away. I remember some hospital administrator, an enormous woman in a flowered dress that made her look a lot like a sofa, had rushed out from behind her glass window to create a diversion. Mother was screaming that doctors were vultures feeding off people's pain, and at that point the woman put her hand on Mother's arm and offered to say a rosary for Grandma, to which Mother said, 'Don't you go Hail-Mary-ing over my mother!'

Then we were rushing away from the doctors and the sofa-lady, and the long hall that would have led us back to Grandma was getting longer and smaller behind us. The hospital doors hissed open, and the wet heat swamped over us. I remember that Mother needed a dishtowel to hold the steering wheel.

She didn't cry that day, though we tried to make enough quiet in the car to permit crying. Oh, at first I had climbed in the back seat babbling about wanting a towel to sit on and being thirsty, but Lecia had a way of grabbing a hold of me with a look that shut down any of my whining in a heartbeat's time. Her brown eyes sloped down at the corners, and the bangs above them were hairsprayed into a row of shiny blonde spikes. She could always nail me with that look and make me stop mid-sentence. In the small rear-view mirror, Mother's eyes were eerily blank. Nothing showed in them but the road's white dashed lines, which seemed to be flying off the asphalt like knives and into the darkest part of her pupils where they disappeared .

After the amputation and that trip to Houston, we didn't see Mother much. She either came home from the hospital briefly in the mornings to change clothes before heading back, or returned after we were in bed. I would wake to her weight tilting our mattress, her Shalimar settling over me when she leaned in to kiss me and pull up the chenille bedspread. A few times, she would sit on my side of the bed all night smoking, till the yellow light started in the windows. She had a way of waving away the smoke from my face and making a pleasant little breeze in the process. I kept my eyes closed, knowing that if I roused she'd leave, and I wanted nothing more from her on those nights than to let me lie in the mist of that perfume I now wear and to imagine the shapes her Salem smoke made. Inside the great deep pit that I had begun digging in my skull, I had buried the scariness of Grandma's hacked-off leg. I could feel through the bedspread the faint heat of my mother's body as she sat a few inches from where I lay, and that heat was all I needed.

Except for these apparitions of Mother, we were left the rest of the summer in Daddy's steady if distracted care. At some point, his friends started to arrive in pick-ups with tool boxes to turn our garage into an extra bedroom for my parents, who had been sleeping on a pull-out sofa in the living-room during Grandma's visit. Each morning, about the time that Lecia and I reached the bottom of our soggy Cheerios, somebody's work boots would stamp up the porch steps, and the screen would bang open and Daddy would start getting down clean coffee mugs.

The men arrived early and worked steadily through the hottest part of every day. They had all taken their vacations then in order to help out. They worked for nothing but free coffee and beer. By mid-morning they had stripped off their shirts. They had broad backs and strong arms, and suffered the fiercest sunburns that summer I ever remember seeing. Bill Engman had a round hairless beer belly that pooched over his carpenter apron, and his back burned and skin peeled off in sheets then burned again until it finally darkened to the colour of cane syrup. The men pulled Lone Star beers all afternoon from the ice in two red Coleman coolers that Daddy packed to the brim every morning.

A few times a day, somebody's wife would show up with food. Say what you like about the misery of hard labour—I once had a summer job painting college dorms that I thought would kill me—it can jack up your appetite to the point where eating takes on a kind of holiness. Whether there were white bags of barbeque crabs from Sabine Pass or tamales in corn husks from a roadside stand, the men would set down their tools and grin at the sheer good fortune of it. They always took time to admire the food before they started to eat, a form of modesty I guess, or appreciation, as if wanting to be sure the meal wouldn't vanish like some mirage. Daddy would stop to soak his red bandanna in a cooler's slush and study whatever was steaming out of the torn open sack while he mopped himself off. 'Lord God, look at that,' he'd say, and wink at whoever had brought it.

Bill's wife, Pearl, pulled in once with a wash-tub of sandy unshucked oysters that it took two men to heave out of the truck-bed. She spent the better part of a morning opening them with a stubby knife. When she was done, there were two huge pickle jars of cleaned oysters sitting in the wash-tub's cold water. We ate them with hot sauce and black pepper and lemon. (Lecia says that I would eat them only in pairs, so none would feel lonely in my stomach.) The oysters had a way of wincing when you squeezed lemon on them. They started off cold in your mouth but warmed right up and went down fast and left you with a musty aftertaste of the sea. You washed that back with a sip of cold beer you'd salted a little. And you followed that with a soda cracker.

Before that summer, I had many times heard long-winded Baptist preachers take ten minutes to pray over card-tables of potato salad and fried chicken at church picnics, but the way those sweating, red-faced men sat around on stacked pallets of lumber gulping oysters taught me more of what I know about simple gladness. At evening, they would pull off their work boots, peel off their double layers of cotton socks and lay them to dry across the warm bricks. Daddy tipped the beer coolers out where they stood in the grass, and cold water rushed over their feet. At that time of day, with night coming in fast, and the men taking a minute to pass a pint of Tennessee whiskey between them or light their smokes, there was a glamour around them that I sensed was about to disappear. When they climbed into the cabs of their trucks, I had a terrible urge to rush after them and call them back.

By August, my folks had a panelled bedroom with a separate tiled shower. At the back of the house, there stood a detached garage big enough for two cars. It also held a separate work studio for Mother, my father's one nod to her desire to paint. The studio had a high ceiling and skylights and a black stove where she could build a fire on a rainy night. She wasted no time setting up her easel and starting to work in oils. The first thing she did was a portrait of Grandma wearing a plain blue dress. She worked from a Polaroid taken just before Grandma lost the leg.

Mother must have worked on it late at night after she came in from the hospital. God knows she had no other time. She'd even given up her job at the local paper to nurse Grandma. But the amber-coloured sketch that first appeared on the white canvas turned into a facsimile of my grandmother inside of a week. I snuck the studio key off the nail in the kitchen to check its progress every few days. When I pulled the padlock off and the studio door swung open, I felt like a thief in church. I was entering a realm that had before only filled Mother's bedtime stories of great artists: Van Gogh's lopped-off ear; Gaugin's native girls; the hump-backed Degas mad for love of his dancers; how Pollock once paid a fortune for a Picasso drawing, then erased it in order to see how it was made. The combination of turpentine and damp woodsmoke and the distant sting of vodka was unlike any other batch of smells before or since. The whole idea of erecting a person—from tinted oil and whatever swirled inside my mother's skull—filled me with a slack-jawed wonder.

The portrait of Grandma wound up stiffer, more formal than Mother's other work. The arms bend at right angles. The shoulders are square like a military man's, and the face is totally devoid of feeling. Perhaps it was that blankness that I was trying to erase when I squirted orange paint on to a sable brush and dabbed at the mouth. Maybe I was trying to blot her out somehow, or shut her up. If you'd asked me at the time, I think I would have said I was trying to brighten her lipstick. Ultimately, though, all I did was leave an orange blotch in the middle of the painting's face.

Mother wept when she saw it and cursed the ignorant vandals who had broken in. She never even asked whether one of us had done it. She got drunk wearing a Mexican serape and built a fire and cursed the Mother-Fucking Swamp and its occupants. *They do not*, she told us with terse judgement, *even deserve to call themselves members of the chordate phylum*, which Lecia had to explain meant that they didn't have spinal columns and were, therefore, like worms, slugs and leeches. The next morning, Mother bought a stout lock you couldn't get through with any bolt cutter. The new key stayed on the same kitchen nail, but after that I was afraid of wrecking something else and so stayed out of the studio.

When Grandma came back to our house she had ossified into something elemental and really scary. She seemed way thinner than she had been in the hospital, though perhaps not as pale. She had been fitted with an artificial leg that she strapped on every morning. It wore a sturdy black shoe that never came off. At night, she detached the leg and stood it by her bed. Once, when I passed her door on my way to the toilet, I caught sight of it standing there with no person tacked on top, casting a long shadow into the hall that nearly reached my bare feet. The honeysuckle that grew up our screens made spiky wall-shadows on nights like that. Sometimes I'd hear Grandma hop down the short hall into the bathroom, her cane whacking the door moulding. Lecia says that I misremember one specific sight of her standing in our doorway with that stump bluntly hanging down under her nightie, her arms spread so she could hold herself up by the doorjambs and her hair fanned out around her face like white fire.

Grandma wore very pale pink, nylon pyjamas with a matching robe, and her wheelchair was spookily silent in the way somebody walking never was. With Daddy's Three-In-One oil and her own maniacal patience she kept it tuned silent. She'd up-end the chair by her bed and squirt oil in all the tiny hollow places so it was nothing but glide. Then she could materialize soundlessly around a corner. She had a habit of sneaking up on Lecia and me and shouting *Aha!* as if she'd discovered us shooting up heroin with a turkey baster. Once she found us playing gin rummy and let out her *Aha!* and then called Mother. She watched us the whole time she was yelling, as if we were going to cover up the cards before Mother got there. 'Charlie Marie! Come in here and whip these children. I swear to God . . . ' Mother, who never excelled as a spanker, arrived and asked some bewildering questions. Grandma gave an evangelistic-sounding lecture on the evils of gambling and liquor, this despite the fact that she'd been an avid cheat at church bingo and was, since her surgery, consuming about a case of beer every day. After a while, Mother gave in to Grandma's rantings and went through the motions of flailing at our legs with a fly swatter till we ran into our room and slammed the door. I remember crawling up in Lecia's lap and whining about how I hadn't done anything. Lecia reasoned that we'd probably got away with fifty things we should have been spanked for that day, so we should just call it even.

In August I started walking in my sleep. Actually I did things other than just walk: I'd squat and go to the bathroom behind the living-room drapes leaving a pile that my parents sometimes didn't find till morning. Once I wandered outside, and Daddy had to come chasing after me.

That fall my school career didn't go well either. I got suspended from my second-grade class twice, first for biting a kid named Phyllis who wasn't to my mind getting her scissors out fast enough to comply with the teacher's instruction; then again for breaking my plastic ruler over the head of a boy named Willy Don Smitts, whom I adored. I remember the blue knot rising through the blond stubble of his crew cut. Both times I got sent to the principal, a handsome ex-football coach named Frank Doleman who let Lecia and me call him Uncle Frank. (Lecia and I had impressed Uncle Frank by learning to read more or less without instruction before we were three. Mother took us down to his office in turn, and we each dutifully read the front page of the day's paper out loud to him, so he could be sure it wasn't just some story we'd memorized.)

He let me stay in his office playing chess all afternoon with whoever wandered in. He loved pitting me against particularly lunk-headed fifth- and sixth-grade boys who'd been sent down for paddlings they never got. He'd try to use my whipping them at chess to make them nervous about how dumb they were. 'Now this little bitty old second-grader here took you clean in six plays.

Don't you reckon you need to be listening to Miss Formino instead of cutting up?' When Mrs Helms led me solemnly down the hall to Frank Doleman's office, I would pretend to cry, but I remember thinking about Brer Rabbit from Uncle Remus as he was being thrown into the briar patch where he'd been born and raised, screaming, *Please don't throw me in that briar patch!* At the end of both days, Uncle Frank drove me home himself in his white convertible, the waves of kids parting as we passed, and me flapping my hand at all of them like I was Jackie Kennedy.

It was also at this time that I came to be cut out of the herd of neighbourhood kids by an older boy. Obviously I had some kind of fear or hurt on me that an evil boy can smell. He knew I could be drawn aside and scared or hurt a little more than the others. Before that happened there was almost something sacred about that pack of kids. No matter how strange our family was thought to be, we blended with the tribe when we all played together. For some reason, I always remember us running barefoot down the football field together, banking and turning in a single unit like those public television airplane shots of zebras in Africa.

There were dozens of us. We ranged in age from thirteen or fourteen for the big boys down to Babby Allen, who at two trailed behind the herd everywhere. I was seven and small-boned and skinny, but more than able to make up for that with sheer meanness. Daddy had instructed me in the virtue of what he called 'equalizers', which meant not only sticks and rocks but having a long memory for mistreatment. I wouldn't hesitate to sneak up blindside and bite a bigger kid who'd got the better of me a week before. (To this day, I don't know whether to measure this as courage or cowardice, but it stuck. After I grew up, the only man ever to punch me found himself awakened two nights later from a dead sleep by a solid right to the jaw, after which I informed him that, should he ever wish to sleep again, he shouldn't hit me.)

In some ways, the kids in my neighbourhood were identical. Our fathers belonged to the same union ('Oil Chemical and Atomic Workers, Local 1242' was how they answered the phone on Daddy's unit). They punched the same clocks for almost exactly the same wage. (Our family had been considered 'rich' because of Mother's part-time newspaper work.) Maybe one kid's daddy worked at Gulf and another at Texaco and another at Atlantic-Richfield, but it amounted to the same thing. Maybe one was a boilermaker and another controlled the flow of catalyst in a cracking unit, but they all worked turning crude oil into the various by-products you had to memorize by weight in seventh-grade science class—kerosene, gasoline and so on. The men all worked shifts because that paid a little better, so all of us knew to tiptoe on days when the old man was on graveyards. The union handed out little cardboard signs that ladies tacked to their doors reading: 'Shhh! Shift Worker asleep.' Nobody but Mother had ever been to college (she'd attended both Texas Tech and art school).

On hot days, when running was forbidden—heatstroke was always bringing a little kid down—we played a game called 'Torture'. It was invented by the older boy I mentioned. He would cram us into the skin-tightening heat of the most miserably close spot we could find—the spidery crawl-space under the Smitts' back porch, say, or Jerry Fontenot's old pigeon cage or some left-over refrigerator box waiting for the garbage truck. There, we would squat into the hunched and beaten forms we thought made us look like concentration camp inmates. This particular boy had a picture of Buchenwald survivors in his history book. All of us memorized it; not out of any tender feeling for the victims' pain or to ponder injustice, but so we could impersonate them when playing Torture. We lined up shoulder to shoulder and thigh to thigh under the cool blue eye of this big boy's Nazi. He didn't twist arms or squish heads or inflict wounds. He was too smart for that. He just reigned over us while our parents called us home for lunch. We hunkered down without moving. Blinking or whimpering wasn't permitted. We melted into a single compliant shape. It was almost a form of meditation. The world slowed down, and your sense of your own body got almost unbearably distinct. I remember how sweat rivered down my ribcage. I could feel every particle of grit in the fold of my neck. Eventually, of course, some adult arm would poke into where we were hiding, signalling the arrival of somebody's mom come to pull us out and drag us home for lunch or supper.

And it was one of these times—an evening oddly enough—when the arm felt around and didn't find me huddled in the corner, that all the other kids poured and scattered to their separate homes for supper, so this big boy and I were left alone.

It was going dark when he got hold of me under God knows what pretext. He took me into somebody's garage. He unbuttoned my white shirt and told me I was getting breasts. Here's what he said: 'You're getting pretty little titties now, aren't you?' I don't recall any other thing being said. He pulled off my shorts and underwear and threw them in the corner in a ball, over where I knew there could be spiders. He pushed down his pants and put my hand on his thing, which was unlike any of the boys' jokes about hot dogs and garden hoses. It was hard as wood and felt as big around as my arm. He wrapped both my hands around it and showed me how to slide them up and down; it felt like a wet bone encased in something. At some point, he tired of that. He got an empty concrete sack and lay it down on the floor and me down on top of that and pumped between my legs till he got where he was headed. I remember I kept my arms folded across my chest, because the thing he'd said about my breasts was such an obvious lie. It made me feel ashamed. I was seven and a good ten years from having anything like breasts. My school record says I weighed less than fifty pounds. Think of two good-sized Smithfield hams—that's about how big I was. Then think of a hundred and thirty-some-odd pounds of newly erect teenaged boy on top of that and pumping between my legs. It couldn't have taken very long.

(I picture him now reading this, and long to reach out of the page and grab a hold of his shirt front so that we might reminisce some. Hey Bucko, probably you don't read, but you must have somebody who reads for you, your pretty wife or some old neighbour boy you still go fishing with. Or your mother, who speaks so kindly to me when I visit home that I've kept my mouth shut these thirty years for fear of killing her with news of what you are. Where will you be when the news of this paragraph floats back to you? For some reason, I picture you lying under your sink tinkering with plumbing. Your wife will mention that in some book I wrote, somebody from the neighbourhood is accused of diddling me at seven. Maybe your head will click back a notch as this registers. Maybe you'll see your face's image spread across the silver U-joint pipe like it's been flattened by a ballpeen hammer. Probably you thought I forgot what you did, or you figured it was no big deal. I say this now across decades and thousands of miles solely to remind you of my long memory, and of the deep mean streak that your dear, ageing mother always said I had.)

When he was done with me it was full dark. I unballed my clothes and tried to brush off the insects. He helped me to dress. He tied my Keds for me. He washed me off with the faucet that came out from the side of somebody's house; the water was warm from being in the pipe on a hot day, and my legs were still sticky after.

Our porch light was amber. The rest of the houses were dark. You could see the spotlights from the Little League Park and hear the loudspeaker announcing somebody at bat. I wondered if this boy had planned to get a hold of me in advance, if he'd picked the time when everybody would be at the game. The idea that he'd consciously chosen to do this, then tracked me down like a rabbit, made me feel sick. He walked me home not saying anything, like he was doing a babysitting chore.

I stood on my porch by myself. I could hear his tennis shoes slapping away down the street. I watched the square of his white T-shirt get smaller till it disappeared around the corner.

The honeysuckle was sickly sweet that night. I stood outside for a long time. I tried to arrange my face into nothing special having happened. There was a grey wasp's nest in the corner of our porch. It had chambers like a honeycomb, each with the little worm of a baby wasp inside, sleeping. I thought sleeping that way would be good. After a while, Daddy pulled open the door and shoved the screen open and asked me had I been at the game. I still fitted under his armpit walking in. 'Come in, Pokey, lemme fix you a plate,' he said. You could hear a roar from the park as somebody turned a double-play or got a hit. I thought of the boy climbing the bleachers towards his admirers. I thought of all the jokes I'd heard about blow jobs and how a girl's vagina smelled like popcorn.

I looked at my father, who would have climbed straight up those bleachers and gutted this boy like a fish, and at my mother, who for some reason I imagined bursting into tears and locking herself in the bathroom over the whole thing. Grandma in her wheelchair would have said she wasn't surprised at all. Lecia was at the game, probably at the top of the bleachers combing down her bangs with a rat-tail comb and laughing when this boy came climbing towards her. He didn't even have to threaten me to keep quiet. I knew what I would be if I told.

GRANTA

CHARLES GLASS
THE BANK MANAGER

In the south of France, at the edge of a cove that cannot be reached by road, lives an old woman from England. She has been there since the end of the war, when most of the beaches were without roads, and most of the people without cars. She has few friends, and the locals call her 'the old Englishwoman who swims in winter.' Every day, winter and summer, she walks across the sand and into the sea, gently treading the water until she is a half mile out, then turning and swimming back. In a white bathing-cap and one-piece suit, she always seems graceful as she floats along. For a few months about four years ago, I was her neighbour. She was eighty then.

I rented the chalet at the end of the garden, where I cooked my own meals and wrote outside on the patio. When I got bored, I would take long swims, much faster and less graceful than Annie's. In the evenings, Annie would usually invite me for a cup of tea or glass of wine. We would sit at a round table where, in disconnected episodes, she told me the story of her life. Her husband had brought her to the south of France just after the war, following a scandal in which he left his wife of many years. I had never heard a woman speak with such love of a man. He was twenty-five years older than she was, and he had died ten years before my arrival. She was entirely unsentimental. Her husband was a scholar, who spent his days translating Greek and Latin poetry, saving much of it for her, sometimes putting little poems he would write himself in the pages of any book she was reading. Every Wednesday, as I recall, he would leave her flowers and a new poem. And he told her one thing I shall not forget: he said that the light shimmering across the sea on a moonlit night, that reflection of the moon that leads from the shore to the horizon, was 'Annie's pathway to the stars.' They were both atheists.

Sometimes, when we sat and talked, Gérard would join us. Annie had explained to me how she had first met Gérard. One morning, just beyond the wall that enclosed her villa and garden, she had seen the sleeping figure of a man on the beach. She noticed him every day or two for a week, and it was obvious he was not eating. She picked some tomatoes from one of the planted terraces behind the house and took them to the sleeping

Gérard. 'The tomatoes grow so beautifully here.'

Gérard had seemed drunk. He accepted the food without a word. Annie walked back through the gate to her garden, sat at the round table under the pergola covered in bougainvillaea and observed him washing the tomatoes in the sea. 'I thought he was a clean enough man, that he cared to wash what he ate.' Later, she had offered him a place to sleep within the walls, high up on one of the terraces behind her villa, in a little wooden chalet on stilts. It had one room with a small bed and was screened all round, but it had no water. He accepted. In time, he had moved down to the larger chalet, made of stone, on the lowest terrace closest to the beach—the chalet I stayed in. It faced Annie's villa from the far end of the garden. It had a kitchen, a bathroom and a porch.

It was Annie's doctor, an old man of Spanish descent, who had suggested she invite Gérard to move into her villa. She was nearly eighty then, and 'old Bartolo', as Annie called the doctor, worried that the chalet was too far away for Gérard to hear Annie if she fell or had an accident. Gérard took the upstairs bedroom next to Annie's. He had by then become her maintenance man, painting the house and chalets, repairing the green shutters when they broke, mending the plumbing and so on. It was then I met him, when he was as much a fixture of the place as the dogs, the cats, the tomato plants, the olive trees, the bougainvillaea, the descending terraces and Annie herself.

Gérard had the face of a hard drinker, and I took him to be ten or fifteen years older than me. He was a nice man, kind but not obsequious, someone who stayed out of the way. When he sat with us on the terrace he never shared our wine, and he did not like tea. He would have a tumbler of water or a cup of coffee. He understood the English we spoke to each other, but he always spoke to us, as we did to him, in French. Perhaps he thought it undignified to speak English, especially with a thick accent, leaving himself open to the same little mistakes that I make in French. I doubt many French people understand how gentle their accent in English is to our ears. Mostly, he sat quietly while Annie talked. Perhaps he had heard her stories before or perhaps he realized she was telling me things she would not tell him.

Gérard preferred impersonal topics, giving me advice about

the movies at the local cinema, the better bars for dragging chicks, nice wines from the south that went well with lamb. I had no telephone and would receive my occasional calls at Annie's. Gérard would walk across the garden, through the little fence that separated my garden from Annie's, to tell me when someone was calling. He would come to the door and shout, '*Téléphone* . . .' uninterested if it were my publisher, pleased in a paternal way when he could add, '*une jeune fille, je crois.*' I left the south of France in the autumn, the manuscript of my book completed, and lost track of him.

The next summer I returned with my wife, our children and my nephew for a holiday. Gérard had never talked much to me, but he was unusually remote during my stay that year. I do not know whether this was because I had a family with me or because his circumstances had changed. I left again and heard nothing more about Gérard until, this year, I called some friends in France who knew Annie and told me her 'handyman' had died.

Annie had not aged when I went to visit. She must be eighty-five now, and she walks slowly—no more slowly, though, than she did before. The mangy dogs barked when I walked into the garden, and they continued barking until boredom overtook them and they lay down in the sun to gnaw at fleas. Annie was neither delighted nor irritated by my intrusion, but she was interested in talking again. She made tea, while I sat in the garden and watched the sea. It was a warm day for winter, but no one was swimming. A young woman walked her dog, and a few children were having a picnic at the other end of the beach where the nudists came in summer. Annie returned with a tray and poured out the tea.

A few weeks ago, she had fallen on one of the boulders just beyond the shore. Old Bartolo ordered her to suspend her daily swim for a few months, which irritated her. She told me a little about her family in England, one of whom I'd met, nothing of consequence. Life had not changed along the beach, she said. The mayor had tried to build a road to it, but local opposition had been too fierce.

I told her I knew Gérard died, but I did not know how. She

repeated the story of her acquaintance with him, how she had seen him on the beach and offered him the tomatoes. She added details I had not known when I was their neighbour. She told of Gérard's despair when he discovered his wife had been having an affair in Paris. It depressed him and unhinged him. The wife used to leave her bank manager husband and their dreary provincial town to make frequent trips to Paris. Later, he learned that a man in Paris had made her his mistress. I don't know, and Annie did not say, whether his wife had confessed to him or he had come across this knowledge in the usual way—a letter, a book of matches in her handbag, a lie that aroused his suspicions, the loss of affection. But he hesitated. He decided to take his wife back. 'But this woman wanted him to join the Communist Party.' Annie was incredulous at the thought. She was not especially anti-communist—she had worked for the Labour Party before she left England—and would have been just as disapproving if the wife had asked Gérard to become a Catholic or practise witchcraft. 'Gérard told me he could not join the Party to get his wife back, because he just didn't believe in it.' So their childless marriage ended, and Gérard left the bank and his house, deserted the faithless wife and took to the road. How many lonely, drunken men have done the same over the centuries, when all the certainties in their lives deserted them? I have seen them in America and England. I used to hang around the railroad yards with hobos when I was thirteen. When one offered me a swig of cheap wine, I felt honoured. That was about the time a song called 'King of the Road' was a hit. My fascination with them lasted a year.

Annie said that a while after I left Gérard had begun an affair with her friend Tamara. She was much younger than Annie, but only a few years older than Gérard. Annie said they had a hopeful time together. Gérard went on living in Annie's villa, taking care of the house and grounds—although the old gardener took care of the terraces and the tomatoes—and waiting there for the day Annie fell or had a stroke. Occasionally, he would spend the night at Tamara's—she never slept at Annie's—returning early in the morning to have breakfast with Annie after her swim. It was not a marriage that he had with Tamara, any more than Annie was a family, but he seemed content.

One morning, as Annie was sitting at her desk, 'going over my papers,' as she put it, Tamara rang. Gérard was outside, working in the garden. 'I didn't want to hear it,' she said, knowing I could not imagine she would eavesdrop, 'but if I hang up the telephone upstairs, the line cuts off.' Gérard went into the house and took the call downstairs in the kitchen. Annie left her telephone on her desk and went back to her papers. Every day, she goes over her husband's notebooks, his articles and his journals, preparing them for her death, when they will need to be in some sort of order if anyone else—they had no children—is to preserve them. When I was living there, she showed me some of his essays and his poems. He was an original thinker, a rationalist with a romantic impulse that Annie must have made him see. She would read through the papers, organize them, bind the notebooks, put them into thematic or chronological order. She was going through one of her husband's essays while Tamara and Gérard had their conversation.

'She told him that if he did not stop drinking, she would leave him,' she said, sitting in the garden below the room in which she overheard that short exchange in French. 'I knew he was not drinking. He had not taken a drink in years. He told her that, but she wouldn't believe him. What could he say?' Finally, they hung up, and Annie put her telephone back.

Annie then heard a sound, like a fall or a crash, from the kitchen, where the downstairs telephone was. She went down the steep stairs of the stone villa to find Gérard lying on the floor. It is no easy task for a woman in her eighties, even one as healthy as Annie, to lift a grown man and carry him to a sofa in an adjoining room. She did it. 'I didn't know I was that strong, but they say in an emergency you find the strength you need.' She called the doctor, old Bartolo, who years before had advised her to take Gérard into her house for her protection. Old Bartolo came, examined Gérard and summoned an ambulance. The ambulance men had a long walk down the hill, through a tunnel and along the beach to the gate of the villa. They covered Gérard in a blanket and tied him on to a stretcher before carrying him nearly a mile to the road. Gérard was dead before they reached the ambulance.

Gérard's family came down from central France for his funeral and they invited Annie. 'I didn't go. I did everything I could for

Gérard when he was alive. As far as I was concerned, there was nothing else to do.' After the funeral, Gérard's brother came to the house, walking down the rocks and along the beach to her gate. He told her, and he was the first person from Gérard's family she had met, that the only time in his life that his brother had been happy was during his years with her. All his life Gérard had been unlucky. I thought it odd that Annie should use the word 'unlucky'. I suppose it was the word the brother used.

Gérard was one of ten children, four boys and six girls. Their father, a canny old peasant farmer, had promised the children—he had not been to school himself—that the first of them to pass the baccalaureate would go on to university at his expense. Although Gérard was not the oldest, he worked to complete his secondary education before any of the others. His older brother had quit school to work the farm, and his sisters had married young. When Gérard passed with distinction, he won a place at the Sorbonne. He went to his father, proudly, to tell him of his achievement and claim his reward. The old man acted surprised. He told Gérard that if he wanted to go to university he would have to pay for it himself. Did he think it would make him a better farmer? Annie did not ask whether the father had forgotten his pledge, had run out of money or had planned all along to play a cruel joke on whichever turned out to be the most ambitious of his children. Gérard left home and went to work in a bank. He was forty-six when he died.

I had assumed that Gérard was much older. He treated me as an older man would, indulgently advising me about French women and wines. He had one of those old Gallic faces that had been through life's war and bore the scars of a thousand little battles. The drink and tobacco added years and crags. His hair was dark though, the thick, wavy hair of a young actor. He was thin and looked strong, and he seemed confident of himself. He did not behave with the humility of a man who had ruined his life and taken refuge with an old woman by the sea. During his years at the bank, I assumed he worked his way from messenger to teller to manager. It was a notable accomplishment for a peasant's son, a hard-working boy who had not been to university. He had become respectable, the man in a suit whom farmers would ask

73

for loans, when his wife abandoned him. In the meantime, his father died hating his bourgeois son, refusing to see him. Gérard's brothers and sisters remained in the countryside, hearing from him only rarely.

They buried Gérard in a churchyard in the south of France, but I doubt anyone will visit. Annie told me that Tamara had begun an affair with someone else two weeks after he died. His brothers and sisters live too far away to bring flowers to his tombstone. His wife is long forgotten, and he had no children. Annie does not visit the dead and plans to have her remains burned to ashes and scattered. Where, I wonder, did his luck run out? If his father had kept the promise, and he had gone to the Sorbonne, might he have been at the barricades in Paris in May of 1968? Might he have become the communist that women like his wife found more intriguing and exciting than the manager of a provincial bank? He was unlucky, I suppose, but his luck might have been worse. He might never have found Annie's beach. He was doing Dr Bartolo's service, waiting patiently to be present when Annie died. He must have dreaded her death more than his own, knowing that her heirs—the uncaring children of her siblings—would sell the villa and send him out of her stone walls, back to the sand where she had found him. Instead, it was he who fell and she who found him. She could not save him from death, but she had saved a small part of his life.

I left Annie in her garden with the dogs and cats, the tomato plants and olive trees, her husband's manuscripts and her fertile memory. Only a few days earlier, my wife had turned me out. I was wandering, as Gérard had done at first. I was not a bank manager, but my wife did not want what I was, a reckless adventurer, equivalent to Gérard's wife's communist, perhaps. No woman can take that, any more she can endure the doom of a provincial bank. What was it Annie and her husband had all those years? What was it that she kept alive? I walked from her garden along the beach, smiling at the young woman with the dog. I made my way to the path and through the tunnel to the road. Driving away, in no particular direction, I said a prayer for Gérard. Perhaps, I thought, I should look after Annie, now that he was gone.

GRANTA

T. CORAGHESSAN BOYLE
LITTLE AMERICA

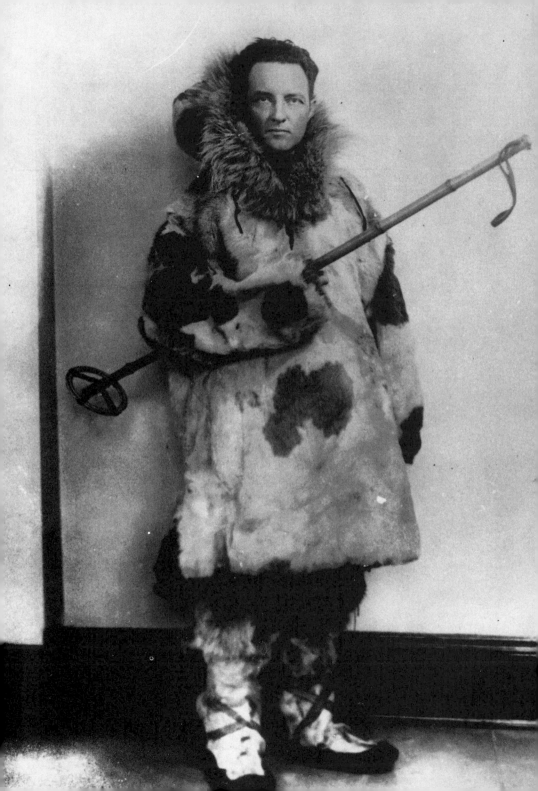

All he wanted was a quarter, fifty cents, a dollar maybe. The guy was a soft touch, absolutely—the softest. You could see it in the way he clutched the suitcase with his big-knuckled hairy old hands and kept blinking his eyes as if he'd just got out of bed or something. People were spilling out of the train, the usual crush—a scrawny black woman with the pale splash of a birthmark on her face and two angry-looking kids clinging to her dress, a tight little clump of pin-eared teenagers, guys with briefcases and haircuts hustling up the ramp with their chop-chop strides—and nobody had spotted the old man yet. Roger stood motionless, twenty feet from him, and waited. Out of the corner of his eye he saw Rohlich holding out his battered Orioles cap to a polyester wonder with sun-glasses like a visor, and he saw the look of annoyance, the firm set of the jaw, the brush-off. Rohlich's voice came back to him like a bad radio over the squeal of the train's brakes and the scrape and clatter of shoes on the pavement and all the birdy jabber of the arriving and departing: 'Hey, who bit you in the ass, man? All I wanted was a quarter—'

But the old man, the softest of touches, never moved. He stood rooted to the floor, just in front of the BALTIMORE sign, his watery old eyes roving over the crowd as if he was an explorer and he'd just discovered a new tribe. The man was old, Roger could see that, seventy at least, and he didn't have a clue as to where he was. Ducking his head and sidling across the floor with the crab-walk he always used on touches—never come up to them directly, never freak them—Roger moved in. He was moistening his lips to make his pitch and thinking, *A buck, a buck at least*, when the old man's face suddenly lit with a smile. Roger looked over his shoulder. There was no one there. The old man was smiling at him.

'Hey,' Roger crooned, ducking his head again and rolling it back on his shoulders, 'hello. I mean, how you doin'?'

He was wearing a suit, the old man, and nothing too shabby either—probably mohair or something like that—and his hair was perfectly parted, a plumb line that showed a swath of naked pink

Photo: Associated Press

Opposite: Rear Admiral Richard E. Byrd, the first man to fly over both North and South Poles and leader of two Arctic and five Antarctic expeditions.

scalp beneath. The skin was drawn tight under his cheek-bones and there was something strange about his lips, but the milky eyes were focused now. On Roger. 'Well, well,' the old man said, and his voice was deep and hearty, with an echo to it, 'good to see you again, a real pleasure.' And he reached out his hand for a shake.

Roger took the hand, a dry, old man's hand, held it a moment and looked into his eyes. 'Yeah, sure. Good to see you too.' He'd begun to wonder if the guy was mental or whatever—he was probably looking for his nurse. Or his keeper. But that watch—that was a Movado, three hundred bucks, easy—and he had a college ring that looked like something. 'Real good,' Roger added, for emphasis.

'Yes,' the old man said, and he smacked his lips and held the suitcase out for Roger to take. Roger could feel his heart going. This was too good to be true, a fantasy in three dimensions and technicolor too. He looked over his shoulder, scanned the place for cops and took the suitcase. 'We'll be at the Sheraton again, then?' the old man asked.

Roger took a deep breath, his eyes uncontainable, a whole hive of bees buzzing around inside his chest—*Just get us out of here*—and said, 'Yeah, the Sheraton. Of course. Just like last time, right?'

The old man tugged at his nose as if he was afraid it might drop off his face. He was studying his shoes. 'Just like last time,' he repeated.

One more look around, and then Roger hunched his shoulders over the suitcase and swung toward the street exit. 'Follow me,' he said.

The train always brought back memories—there was a rhythm to it, a discontinuous flow that seemed to peel back the layers of his mind like growth rings in a tree. One minute he was a boy hunched over the radio with his mother as his father's voice spoke to the whole USA from out of the clasp of the impermeable dark, and then he was a father himself, his step light on the cobbles of Beacon Hill, and then a grandfather, and finally an old man on a train, staring back at himself in the flicker of the window. The train did that to him. It was like a drug, a narcotic, a memory solution leaking drop by drop into his uncertain veins. And that was funny too: He was on a train because he didn't like to fly. Richard Evelyn Byrd III, son of the greatest aviator of them all, and he didn't like to fly. Well, he was old now—he'd had enough of flying when he was a boy. A young man really. He remembered the bright flaring skin of Antarctica, the whole ice shelf shaved close with a razor; felt the jolt of the landing and the hard sharp crack of the skis on the ice just as vividly as if they were beneath him now; saw again the light in his father's eyes and the perfect sang-froid with which he confronted all things, the best and the worst alike.

Leverett had put him on the train in Boston and his daughter-in-law was waiting for him in Washington. He repeated it to himself, aloud, as the car swayed and clicked over the rails. *Leverett. His daughter-in-law. Washington.* But no, that wasn't right. It was that pleasant young man from the Geographic Society, the one who'd been so nice about the rooms at the Sheraton, he was the one. Of course he was. A first-class reception all the way. And that was only as it should be—he, the son of the father, travelling all the way to the nation's capital for the unveiling of the new commemorative stamp honouring the man whose legend would never die, the last of the men in the old mould, the last hero. Yes. And he would talk to them about that— to Walter what's-his-name at the Geographic Society—about his father's museum. He had a reindeer-skin mukluk with him now, in his suitcase, from the 1929 expedition—just to show it to them, just as bait. There was a whole houseful of stuff back in Boston, a shrine, and it was a shame it wasn't on public display, now and permanently—and why not? For lack of a few dollars? They were financing presidents' libraries, weren't they? And paying out welfare and food stamps and whatnot? What would the Byrd Museum take? A million? Two? Well, he had his father's mukluk for them and that was worth a thousand words of pleading and haggling, ten thousand.

And then the train stopped—he felt it lurch at his insides and for an instant he thought he was up in the hard pellucid Antarctic sky all over again, and he even felt the chill of it. But the train stopped, and there was his suitcase, and he got off. Washington

D.C. The capital. He recognized the station, of course he did. But where was his daughter-in-law? Where was the car? Where was that pleasant young fellow from the Geographic Society?

The old man's voice kept nagging at him, a fruity drone that caught and swallowed itself and vomited it all back up again. Why weren't they taking the car? Were they going to walk the whole way? And his daughter-in-law, where was she? But then he'd change the subject as if he wasn't even listening to himself and the next minute he'd be rattling on about what a bracing day it was, just like high summer at the South Pole, ha ha ha, and now he was laughing or choking—it was hard to say which. Roger stayed two paces ahead of him, head down, fingers locked around the handle of the suitcase, and listened to him bluster and wheeze. 'It's not much farther,' he said. 'You'll see your daughter-in-law, she'll be there, and everybody else too. Here, this way,' he said, and he paused to let the old man draw even with him, and then he steered him down the alley out back of the recycling centre.

They were six blocks from the station now, and the throttle of Roger's heart had eased back a bit, but still, with every step he had to fight down the impulse to take the suitcase and run. That would have been the easy way. But he would have been a fool to do it and he knew the game was going to be a whole lot richer if he played it right. If he could just get the old geek into the back of the warehouse, a quiet place he knew where the newspapers were stacked up twenty feet high, he could dig a little deeper. What else did he have besides the watch and the ring? A wallet maybe? Cash? Credit cards?

At the door to the place—a big aluminium garage door that was pried up in the corner just enough to allow a no-waist man holding his breath to slip right on through—the old guy surprised him. He didn't balk at all. Just took a glance at the trash blown up against the concrete block wall as if it was the most ordinary thing in the world, pinched in his gut and followed Roger into the dark echoing vastness of the warehouse.

And that was it: they were safe. It was over. Anything the old man had was Roger's, right on down to his undershorts, and there was nobody to say any different. Roger led him behind a column of newsprint and set the suitcase down. 'Here we are,' he said, turning to face the old man, 'the Sheraton.'

'This isn't the Sheraton,' the old man said, but he didn't seem upset at all. He was grinning and his eyes were bright. 'It isn't the Ritz-Carlton either. You're pulling my leg, aren't you?'

Roger gave him back the grin. There was a long pause during which he became aware of the distant beep-beep-beep of a forklift somewhere on the far side of the warehouse. 'Yeah, sure,' Roger said finally, 'I was only joking, sure I was. Can't fool you, huh?' He settled himself down on a stack of newspaper and motioned for the old man to do the same. He lit a cigarette—or the stub of a cigarette he'd picked out of an ashtray at the station. He was taking his time, enjoying himself—there was no reason to rush, or to get violent either. The old man was out there, no doubt about it.

'So what's in the suitcase?' Roger asked casually, shaking out the match and exhaling through his nostrils.

The old guy had been sitting there, as content as if he was stretched out in his easy chair back at home, smacking his lips and chuckling softly to himself, but now his face went serious. 'My father's mukluk.'

Roger couldn't help himself. He let out a laugh. 'Your father's who?'

'Here, let me show you,' the old man said, and Roger let him take the suitcase. He propped it up on his bony old knees, popped the latches and pulled back the lid to reveal a nest of garments, socks, shirts, handkerchiefs and a tweed sport coat. Rummaging around a moment, he finally came up with what he was looking for—some kind of shoe or boot or something, made out of fur—and held it up for Roger's inspection as if it was the Hope Diamond.

'So what did you say this was?' Roger asked, taking the thing from him and turning it over in his hand.

'My father's mukluk. For the museum.'

Roger didn't know what to make of this. He pulled quietly on his cigarette a moment, then handed the thing back to him with a shrug. 'Is it worth anything?'

'Ha!' the old man boomed, and Roger was afraid he was

going to get to his feet and try something. 'Worth anything? The very mukluk Admiral Byrd wore in *Little America*? The very one?' The old man drew himself up, cradling the shoe to his chest. 'And I tell you something—and you can tell Walter from me,' he said, lowering his voice in confidentiality, 'I've got plenty more where this came from. Plenty. Notebooks, parkas, reindeer pants and finnesko boots, the sun compass itself—the very one he used to make his fix on the Pole.' He rocked back on his haunches. 'Yes,' he murmured, and he might have been talking to himself, so oblivious was he of Roger and his surroundings, 'you tell Walter. All we need is maybe a million. And that's nothing these days. Nothing.'

The old man was as crazy as plantlife, but that only took you so far, and though Roger had nowhere to go—hadn't had anywhere to go in maybe ten years now—he was getting impatient. 'You're absolutely right,' he said, cutting him off in the middle of a windy speech about his museum, and he used the phrase as an excuse to lean forward and shake the dry old hand again. But this time, unlike the first, when every eye in the station was on them, Roger expertly slipped the watch over the bony wrist and dropped it in his coat pocket, and the old man didn't know a thing about it.

Or maybe he did. His expression changed suddenly, as if he was trying to remember something. The lines stood out in his face. He looked old. Old and constipated. 'I'm thirsty,' he suddenly announced.

'Thirsty?' Roger roared, drunk with his own success. 'Hell, so am I—what say we share a pint or two, eh? Have a party. Drink to your mukluk and your museum.' He stood and patted his pockets theatrically, enjoying himself all over again—he couldn't remember the last time he'd had this much fun. 'But I'm a little short—you got any cash? For a drink, I mean?'

Another facial change. The jaw clenched, the eyes caught hold of him. 'You're not the young man from the Geographic Society,' the old man said quietly.

'The hell I'm not,' Roger protested, and he was so frisky all of a sudden he spun around twice and threw out his arms like a tap dancer rising to the finale. 'Sure I am, old man, sure I am—

but listen, what did you say your name was?'

'Byrd. Richard Evelyn Byrd. The Third.'

Oh the solemnity of it, the dignity. He might have been announcing the King of Arabia or something. Roger laughed out loud. 'Bird, huh? Tweet-tweet. Bird the Third.' Then he let a hint of ugliness creep into his voice and he stood over the old man now, no mistaking the posture: 'I said, you got any cash for a drink, Bird the Third?'

The hand shook, the fingers fumbled in the jacket pocket, and there was the wallet, genuine calfskin, receptacle for the sort of notes and documents that separated people like the old man from Roger and Rohlich and all the other bleary-eyed, rotten-toothed bums and winos curled up on their sheets of cardboard across the city. In that moment, Roger almost felt sorry for the old retard—almost. But in the end, of course, he felt sorrier for himself, and in a quick swipe the wallet was his: five twenties, folded and joined with a paper clip, three ones, a return ticket, Washington to Boston. Photos: an old lady, a kid in a little league outfit, some white-haired old duffer in a parka. And what was this, what was this?! A Visa card, thin as a wafer, shiny as a pot of gold.

He was used to a cocktail before dinner—a Manhattan, generally, shaken, and with a twist instead of a cherry— and a good cabernet or pinot noir with his meal, but this was something he hadn't experienced before, this was something new. The young man passed him the bottle—GALLO WHITE PORT, the label read, ALCOHOL 19% BY VOLUME—and he took a long gulping swallow that left his chin wet and his stomach burning. He was thirsty, nearly parched, and the liquid—it was cold, it was wet—went down easily, and after the first drink he didn't care what it was. When the bottle was gone, the young man produced another, and though he'd been hungry, though he hadn't eaten anything except the egg salad sandwich and the apple his son had given him at the Boston station, the hunger faded and he felt better and better as the evening wore on. He was telling the young man about pemmican, how it was the highest-energy food man had yet to devise and how many calories you had to replace daily just to stay alive at seventy-five below, when all at once he felt as lucid as he ever had. He caught himself up so suddenly he almost choked. This wasn't the young man from the Geographic Society, not at all. There was the same fringe of patchy, youthful beard, the startled blue eyes and delicate raw skin, but the nose was all wrong and the mouth had a mean, hurtful look to it. And his clothes—they were in tatters, soaked through with the grease and leavings of the ages, reeking, an unforgivably human stink he could smell from all the way over here. 'This isn't Washington,' the old man said, understanding now that he'd gotten off at the wrong stop, that he was in some other city altogether, a place he didn't know, understanding that he was lost. 'Is it?'

His face shining with drink, his ragged arms flailing at the air, the young man howled with manic glee, kicked at the newspapers heaped up round him and finally had to clutch his ribs tight to stop the laughter. He laughed till he began to cough, and he coughed till he brought something up and spat it on the floor. 'You are out there, Bird,' he said, straining at each word, and the laughter seized him again. 'You are really out there.'

So: he was lost. It had happened to him before, two or three times at least. A trick of the mind, that was all, one little mistake—getting off at the wrong stop, turning right instead of left—and the world became a strange and unfathomable place, terrain to explore all over again. He didn't mind. They'd come for him, Leverett and his wife, sweet girl really, and the grandchildren, they'd find him. But then a little wedge of concern inserted itself along the fracture lines of his psyche, and it became a worry. Who was this man if he wasn't from the Geographic Society, and what did he want? And what was this place? Newspapers. Drifts of them, mountains, a whole continent, and all it was was newsprint.

He took the bottle when it came to him and he took a drink and passed it back, and there was a third member of their party now, another hand interposed between him and the young man who wasn't from the Geographic Society. Matted beard, nose like a bird of prey, eyes frozen into his head, and he didn't know him, not at all, but why did he look so familiar? He felt himself drifting. It was cold, damnably cold, for what—October, wasn't it? 'Early winter this year,' he murmured, but no one uttered a word in response.

The next time he noticed anything, it was the candle. He must have dozed. But there it was, the candle. A light in the wilderness. The bottle came back to him and the feeble light leapt out suddenly to illuminate the new man's face and he knew him, knew him as well as he knew his own son and his own father. 'You,' he said out of the void, 'I know you.'

There was a low cackle, a dribble of hard-edged laughter from two ravaged throats. 'Yeah, we know you too, Bird the Third,' the young man said, and his voice had changed, the tone of it, till everything he said sounded like a schoolyard taunt.

'No,' the old man insisted, 'not you . . . I mean'—and he looked the newcomer full in the face—'I mean you.' The inspiration had flared in his brain, and he knew the man even after all these years, a great man, his father's equal almost, the only other man in the world who'd been to both Poles and back again. 'You're Roald Amundsen.'

The laugh was ugly, almost a bark. The man showed the stubs of his teeth. He took his time, drinking, wiping his mouth with the back of his sleeve. 'Shit man, sure I am,' he said, and the other one was laughing again, 'and this here, your friend with the bottle, this guy's Santy Claus.'

Roger was on a tear. For a full week, seven whole days and maybe more, he didn't know where he was. He hadn't had this much money, all at once, since he'd left New Jersey, when he was a kid living in that lopsided trailer with his mother and stocking the shelves at Waldbaum's. The whole thing with the old man had been unreal, the sort of score everybody dreams about but never makes, never. Oh, sure, zombies like Rohlich would tell you they were hitch-hiking once and Madonna gave them a lift, or some high roller in Atlantic City handed them a C-note when all they asked for was a quarter, but this was unreal, this *happened*. Those five twenties alone could have kept him flying for a month or more, but of course they'd disappeared, dropped down the hole where all of it went sooner or later—usually sooner. He didn't know where he'd been or what he'd done, but he ached all over, so it must have been good, and he needed a drink so bad he could taste it. Or couldn't taste it. Or whatever.

And shit, it was cold. Too cold for this time of year. Cold and drizzling. When he woke up an hour or so ago he'd found himself on a wet slab of cardboard out back of the fish restaurant the yuppies flocked to—Cicero's—and he didn't know how he'd got there or what he'd done the night before, and his pockets were empty. No loose change. No nothing. He'd wandered over to the mission and passed a short dog around with the black guy they called Hoops, and now he was wet through to the skin and shivering and looking for a benefactor so he could invest in the Gallo Company and warm up where it counted most. He remembered the old guy's watch then, the black Movado, and felt around in his pockets for it. It was gone. He had a further—and dimmer—recollection of pawning it and getting ten bucks for the thing and being all pissed off about it, but then he wasn't so sure—it might have been another watch and another time.

He stayed on the street for a couple hours, it got a whole lot colder, and all he came up with was ninety-two cents. By then, his thirst was driving him crazy, so he bought a can of beer and went over to the warehouse to see who was around and maybe trade up for a hit or two of wine. He saw that somebody had tried to hammer the crease out of the door and that they'd moved a whole shitload of papers out and a whole new shitload in, but other than that nothing had changed. There was nobody around, so he made himself a little igloo out of bundled newspaper, drank his beer in two swallows and tried to stop shivering for a minute at a time.

At first he didn't hear it—or it didn't register. The place was cavernous, with a ceiling you could fly planes under and walls that went on for a block, and it was noisy, middle of the day, trucks rumbling in and out of the South Street entrance with cans and bottles, and Mr and Mrs Nice driving up with Sis and Bud to deliver their neat foursquare string-tied bundles of newspaper. It was noisy and he didn't hear a thing but the muted rumble of all that activity and he wished five o'clock would come and they'd shut the place down and go home and leave him in peace, but after a while he became aware that somebody was there with him, just up the next aisle, muttering to himself in the low sweet sing-song tones of the crack-brained and hopeless. Another bum.

Somebody he knew maybe. A man with a short dog and maybe a bite of something scavenged from the top of the bin out back of the supermarket. He felt his spirits lift.

He pushed himself up, keeping an eye out for the watchman, and slipped up the next aisle. The papers had fallen in drifts here, sloppily stacked, and he fought his way through them in the direction of the voice, his harsh ragged breath crystallizing before him. There was a nook carved out of the wall, and he saw the back of a white head, the old withered stalk of a neck, and there he was: Bird the Third.

He was amazed. He would have thought the guy would be long gone, would have found his people, his keeper, whatever. But still, there he was, and for a moment Roger felt a surge of hope. Maybe he had something on him still, something he'd overlooked, some piece of jewellery, a pair of glasses—hell, his clothes even. But then he saw that they'd already got to him. The old retard's suit was gone, his socks and shoes too. Somebody'd switched on him, and he was dressed in a puke-green janitor's jumpsuit and he was missing a shoe—or he'd found a shoe somewhere, a torn greasy old Nike sneaker with the toes ripped out. He was pathetic. A mess. And he wasn't worth anything to anybody.

For a long while, Roger just stood there watching him. The old man was shivering, his arms wrapped around himself like coils, the bare foot discolored and bad-looking. He had that thousand-mile stare on his face, the same one you saw on some of the older guys, the Vietnam vets and whatnot. Roger's brain was working hard, and for a moment he saw himself taking the guy along to the police station and turning him in like a hero and maybe getting a reward from the guy's family or whoever. They had to be looking for him. You don't come from that world with your haircut and your suitcase and your Movado watch without somebody looking for you, especially if you're a little soft in the head to begin with.

It was a good idea for about eight seconds, and then it became a whole lot less good, and ten seconds further on it just plain stank. There wouldn't be any reward—maybe for Joe Average and Mr and Mrs Nice, maybe for them, but not for the likes of Roger. That's how things worked. There were two worlds operating here, the one where Bird the Third and all the rest of them lived, and this one, the real one, where you slept under things at ankle-level and ate the crumbs they gave you. Well, fuck that. Fuck it. It was just like the credit card. He'd tried it on maybe twenty liquor stores, the ones he knew and the ones he didn't, and nobody took him for Bird the Third, no matter how much ID he showed or how hard he tried. Not the way he looked, no way. He was going to trade the thing for a bottle at this one place—*Here, you want the card, Visa Gold? Keep it*—but then the jerk behind the counter got nasty, real nasty, and confiscated the whole business, plastic, ID and all. That's how it was.

He was going to say something, goodbye or thanks for the ride or whatever, but in the end he decided against it. Somewhere, in some deep tunnel of what used to be his reality and was now somebody else's, he even felt a stab of pity, and worse, guilt. But he comforted himself with the thought that if he hadn't been there at the station, somebody else would have, and any way you looked at it Bird the Third would have wound up plucked. In the end, he just shrugged. Then he made his way off through the drifts, thinking maybe he'd just go on down to the station and check out the trains.

Oh, but it was cold. Cold to the bone. And dry. He knew the irony of it all too well—a shelf made of water, frozen and compacted over the howling eons, and not a drop to drink. It was locked in, unavailable, dry as paper. He shifted position and winced. It was his foot. He'd lost all feeling in it there for a while, but now it came back with a vengeance, a thousand hot needles radiating all the way up his leg to the thigh. That's how it was with frostbite. He'd lose his toes, he knew that, but they'd all lost toes, fingers—the great ones—even the tips of their noses. There were continents to explore, unknown corners to make known, and what was a little discomfort compared to the greatness of that?

He thought of his father in the weather shack where he'd wintered alone, the fear of that eternal blackness closing on him like a fist, alternately freezing and asphyxiating himself on the fumes from the kerosene stove. That was greatness. That was will. That was the indomitable spirit he'd inherited. But still it was cold, terribly, implacably cold, unrelentingly cold, and his foot hurt him and he felt himself drifting off to sleep. That was how it happened, that was how they died out here, numbed by the cold, seduced into sleep and forgetfulness.

He stirred, and he fought it. He beat at his thighs, hammered his hands against the meat of his arms, but he couldn't keep it up, and before long he subsided. He tried to call out, but his voice was gone, and besides, it was the coward's way—his father would never have called out. Never. No, he would have gone on into the grip of that Polar night, never wavering, never halting, on and on, into the dream.

Life. A Guide.

What does the future hold for you?

Rather than looking older with every passing year, will you actually appear younger...thanks to injections of bacteria previously thought deadly? Will you be tossing out your trusty wristwatch and sporting a videophone instead?

And when you put your feet up with a glass of your favourite drink, could it be flavour-enhanced by an electronic nose?

If you're interested in learning today about the life you'll live tomorrow, look no further than New Scientist.

Every week we guide you through the fascinating world of scientific and technical advances… including the new synthetic neuroscience that may enable researchers to build brains from scratch.

We increase your understanding of current affairs by examining the wider issues behind the news. For example, in the light of the Lockerbie disaster, we examine new developments in airport sniffers.

New Scientist is not just for scientists. It's for everyone interested to discover what kind of world science and technology are creating for us.

Let New Scientist be your guide to life. Give yourself a free issue, along with a no-risk introductory subscription.

GRANTA

NADINE GORDIMER
L,U,C,I,E

M y name's Lucie—no, not with a 'y'. I've been correcting that all my life, ever since my name was no longer vocables I heard and responded to like a little domestic animal (*here, puss, puss*) and I learnt to draw these tones and half-tones as a series of outlines: L,U,C,I,E. This insistence has nothing to do with identity. The so-called search for identity bores me. I know who I am. You know well enough who you are: every ridge in a toenail, every thought you keep private, every opinion you express is your form of life and your responsibility. I correct the spelling because I'm a lawyer and I'm accustomed to precision in language; in legal documents the displacement of a comma can change the intention expressed in a sentence and lead to new litigation. It's a habit, my pedantry; as a matter of fact, in this instance it simply perpetuates another orthographic inaccuracy: I'm named for my father's Italian grandmother, and the correct Italian form of the name is Lucia. This had no significance for me until I saw her name on her tomb: LUCIE.

I've just been on holiday in Italy with my father. My mother died a few months ago; it was one of those journeys taken after the death of a wife when the male who has survived sees the daughter as the clone woman who, taken out of present time and place to the past and another country, will protect him from the proximity of death and restore him to the domain of life. (I only hope my father has understood that this was one-off, temporary, a gift from me.) I let him believe it was the other way round: he was restoring something to me by taking me to the village where, for him, I had my origin. He spent the first five years of his life dumped by poor parents in the care of that grandmother, and although he then emigrated to Africa with them and never returned, his attachment to her seems never to have been replaced. By his mother, or anyone else; long after, hers was the name he gave to his daughter.

He has been to Europe so many times—with my mother, almost every year.

'Why haven't you come here before?' I asked him. We were sitting in a sloping meadow on what used to be the family farm of his grandmother and her maiden sisters. The old farmhouse where he spent the years the Jesuits believe definitive had been sold, renovated with the pink and green terrace tiles, curlicue iron railings and urns of red geraniums favoured by successful artisans from the new industrial development that had come up close to the village. The house was behind us; we could forget it, he could forget its usurpation. A mulberry tree shaded the meadow like a straw hat. As the sun moved, so did the cast of its brim. He didn't answer; a sudden volley of shooting did—stuttering back and forth from the hills in cracking echoes through the peace where my question drifted with the evaporating moisture of grass.

The army had a shooting range up there hidden in the chestnut forests, that was all; like a passing plane rucking the fabric of perfect silence, the shots brought all that shatters continuity in life, the violence of emotions, the trajectories of demands and contests of will. My mother wanted to go to art galleries and theatres in great European cities, he was gratified to be invited to speak at conferences in Hong Kong and Toronto, there were wars and the private wars of cartels and, for all I know, love affairs—all that kept him away. He held this self hidden from me, as parents do in order to retain what they consider a suitable image before their children. Now he wanted to let me into his life, to confirm it, as if I had been a familiar all along.

We stayed in the only *albergo* in the village and ate our meals in a dark bar beneath the mounted heads of cerf and mountain goats. The mother of the proprietor was brought to see my father, whom she claimed to remember as a small child. She sniffled, of course, recollecting the three sisters who were the last of a family who had been part of the village so long that—that what? My father was translating for me, but hesitantly; not much is left of his Italian. So long that his grandmother's mother had bred silkworms, feeding them on mulberry leaves from her own trees, and spinning silk as part of the home industry which existed in the region before silk from the Orient took away the market. The church square where he vividly remembered playing was still there and the nuns still ran an infant school where he thought he might have been enrolled for a few months. Perhaps he was unhappy at the school and so now could not picture himself entering that blue door, before us where we sat on a bench beside the church. The energy of roaring motor cycles carrying young workers in brilliantly studded and sequinned wind-breakers to the footwear and automobile parts factories ripped his voice away as he told me of the games drawn with a stick in the dust, the cold bliss of kicking snow about, and the hot flat bread sprinkled with oil and salt the children would eat as a morning snack.

Somewhere buried in him was a blue-pearl, translucent light of candles that distorted 'like water' he said, some figures that were not real people. In the church, whose bells rang the hours tremulously from hill to hill, there were only the scratched tracings of effaced murals; he thought the image must have come from some great event in his babyhood, probably the local saint's-day visit to a shrine in a neighbouring town. We drove there and entered the chapels along the sides of a huge airport-concourse of a basilica—my mother was not a Catholic and this analogy comes to me naturally out of my experience only of secular spaces. There were cruel and mournful oil paintings behind the liquid gouts of votive candlelight; he dropped some coins in the box provided but did not take a candle. I don't know whether the dingy representation of the present snuffed out his radiant image or whether his image transformed it for him. We had strong coffee, and cakes named for the shrine, in an arcade of delicious-smelling cafés opposite. He had not tasted those cakes for fifty-eight years, since Lucie bought them as a treat; we had found the right context for the candles that had stayed alight inside him all that time. The cafés were filled with voluble old men, arguing and gesticulating with evident pleasure. They were darkly unshaven and wore snappy hats. I said: 'If you'd stayed, you'd be one of them,' and I didn't know whether I'd meant it maliciously or because I was beguiled by the breath of vanilla and coffee into the fascination of those who have a past to discover.

At night he drank grappa in the bar with the proprietor and picked up what he could of the arguments of village cronies and young bloods over the merits of football teams, while the television babbled on as an ignored attraction. These grandchildren of the patriarchs blew in on a splendid gust created by the sudden arrest of speed as they cut the engines of their motor cycles. They disarrayed themselves, flourishing aside tinsel-enamelled or purple-luminous helmets and shaking out haloes of stiff curls and falls of blond-streaked locks. They teased the old men, who seemed to tolerate this indulgently, grinningly, as a nostalgic resurrection of their own, if different, wild days.

No women came to the bar. Up in my room each night, I leaned out of my window before bed; I didn't know how long I stayed like that, glitteringly bathed in the vast mist that drowned the entire valley between the window and the dark rope of the alps' foothills from which it was suspended, until the church clock—a gong struck—sent waves layering through the mist that I had the impression I could see undulating silvery, but which I was feeling, instead, reverberating through my ribcage. There was nothing to see, nothing. Yet there was the tingling perception, neither aural nor visual, that overwhelms in the swoon before an anaesthetic whips away consciousness. The night before we went to the cemetery, I was quite drunk with it. The reflection of the moon seeped through the endless insubstantial surface, silence inundated this place he had brought me to; the village existed out there no more than it had ever done for me when I had never sat in its square, never eaten under the glass eyes of timid beasts killed in its chestnut forests and mountains, or sat in the shade of its surviving mulberry tree.

W e had four days. On our last afternoon, he said, 'Let's walk up to the old cemetery.' My mother was cremated—so there was no question of returning painfully to the kind of scene where we had parted with her; still, I should have thought in his mood death was too close to him for him to have found it easy to approach any of its territory. But it seemed this was just one of the directions we hadn't yet taken on the walks where he had shown me what he believed belonged to me, given in naming me.

We wandered up to this landmark as we had to others. He took a wrong turning into a lane where plaster gnomes and a miniature windmill stood on a terrace, and canaries sang for their caged lives, piercingly as cicadas. But he retraced our steps and found the right cartographical signals of memory. There was a palatial iron gateway surmounted by a cross, and beyond walls powdery with saltpetre and patched with moss, the black forefingers of cypress trees pointed. Inside: a vacuum, no breath, flowers in green water, withered.

I had never seen a cemetery like that; tombs, yes, and elaborate tableaux of angels over gravestones—but here, in addition to a maze of these there were shelves and shelves of stone-faced compartments along the inner side of the walls, each with its plaque.

Were the dead stored, filed away?

'When there's no room left for graves, it's usual in this country. Or maybe it's just cheaper.' But he was looking for something.

'They're all here,' he said. We stepped carefully on gravelled alleys between tombstones and there they were, uncles and aunts and sons and daughters, cousins who had not survived infancy and other collaterals who had lived almost a century, lived through the collapse of the silkworm industry, the departures of their grown children to find an unknown called a better life in other countries, lived on through foreign occupation during a war and through the coming of the footwear and automobile parts factories—all looking out from photographs framed under convex glass and fixed to their tombstones. No face was old, or sick, or worn. Whenever it was they had died, here they consorted in the aspect they had had when young or vigorously mature.

There were many Albertos and Giovannis and Marias and Clementinas, but the names most honoured by being passed on were Carlo and Lucia, apparently those of the first progenitors to be recorded. Five or six Lucias, from a child in ringlets to fat matrons inclining their heads towards their husbands, many of whom were buried beside them; and then we came to—he came to—her grave. Her sisters were on either side of her. I couldn't read the rest of the inscription, but LUCIE was incised into the ice-smooth black marble. I leaned to look. Go on, he said, giving me the example of bracing his foot on the block that covered her. Under her oval bubble of glass the woman was composed and smooth-haired, with the pupil-less gaze of black eyes, the slightly distended nostrils and straight mouth with indented corners of strong will, and the long neck, emphasized by tear-drop earrings, of Italian beauties. Her eyebrows were too thick; if she had belonged to another generation she would have plucked them and spoiled her looks. He put his arm on my shoulder. 'There's a resemblance.' I shrugged it off with his hand. If your name is on your tombstone, it's definitive, it's not some casual misspelling. Why wasn't she Lucia, like the others?

'I don't really know—only what I was told by my father and he didn't say much . . . parents in those days . . . the sisters kept their mouths shut, I suppose, and in any case he was away working at the docks in Nice from the age of eighteen . . . Apparently she had also gone to work in France when she was very young—the family was poor, no opportunity here. She was a maid in a hotel, and there's something about her having had a love affair with a Frenchman who used the French version of her name . . . and so she kept it, even when she married my grandfather.'

While he was talking a dust-breeze had come up, sweeping its broom among the graves, stirring something that made me tighten my nostrils. The smell of slimy water in the vases of shrivelled flowers and the curious stagnant atmosphere of a walled and crowded space where no living person breathed—what I had taken in when we entered the place was strengthened by some sort of sweetness. With his left foot intimately weighted against her grave, the way a child leans against the knee of a loved adult, he was still talking: 'There's the other version—it comes from *her* mother, that it was *her mother* who was a maid in Nice and my grandmother was her illegitimate child.' I was looking at the foot in the pump-soled running shoe, one of the pair he had kitted himself out with at the market in Cuneo on our way to the village. 'She brought the baby home, and all that remained of the affair was the spelling of the name.' Dust blew into my eyes, the cloying sweetness caught in my throat and coated my tongue. I wanted to spit. 'What the maiden sisters thought of that, how she held out against them? God knows . . . I don't remember any man in the house, I would have remembered . . . '

The sweetness was sickly, growing like some thick liquor loading the air. We both inhaled it, it showed in the controlled grimace that wrinkled round his eyes and mouth and I felt the same reaction pulling at my own face muscles. But he went on talking, between pauses; in them we neither of us said anything about the smell, the smell, the smell like that of a chicken gone bad at the back of a refrigerator, a rat poisoned behind a wainscot, a run-over dog swollen at a roadside—the stench, stench of rotting flesh, and all the perfumes of the living body, the clean salty tears and saliva, the thrilling fluids of love-making, the scent of warm hair, turned putrid. Unbearable fermentation of the sweetness of life. It couldn't have been her. It could not have been coming to him from her, she had been dead so long, but he stayed there with his foot on her stone as if he had to show me that there was no stink in our noses, as if he had to convince me that it wasn't her legacy.

We left saunteringly, ignoring the gusts of foulness that pressed against us, each secretly taking only shallow breaths in revulsion from the past. At the gate we met a woman in the backless slippers and flowered overall that the local women wore everywhere except to go to church. She saw on our faces what was expressed in hers, but hers was mixed up with some sort of apologetic shame and distress. She spoke to him and he said something reassuring, using his hands and shaking his head. She repeated what she had told him and began to enlarge on it; I stood by, holding my breath as long as I could. We had some difficulty in getting away from her, out beyond the walls where we could stride and breathe.

'A young man was killed on his motorbike last week.'

What was there to say?

'I didn't see a new grave.'

'No—he's in one of the shelves—that's why . . . She says it takes some time, in there.'

So it wasn't the secrets of the rotting past, Lucie's secrets, it was the secret of the present, always present; the present was just as much there, in that walled place of the dead, as it was where the young bloods, like that one, tossed down their bright helmets in the bar, raced towards death, like that one, scattering admiring children in the church square.

Now when I write my name, that is what I understand by it.

THOMAS KERN
PICTURES FROM THE WAR

I met Thomas Kern in the lobby of the Al-Rashid Hotel in Baghdad the morning after the first bombing raid. He and two other photographers had been arrested by the Iraqis, questioned and then released—rattled but safe.

We met again in southern Turkey the following spring. The world was saving the Kurds, and Kern disappeared into the mountains for four months to record what saving the Kurds really meant. He stayed there long after the journalists, the photographers, the television crews and the Minister for Overseas Development, Lady Chalker, in her yellow Wellingtons, got fed up and left them to it.

The last time we met was in Sarajevo at Christmas. Kern was two months into the assignment laid out in these pages. Although we spent long periods in the same places, we rarely ran into each other. When my fellow hacks came together in the Holiday Inn for heat, electricity and a reprieve from the misery, he was not with us. And when the hack pack called greetings to returned friends as they wandered into the dining-room, few knew Thomas Kern.

His pictures are a testimony to his self-imposed exile from the comfort of the familiar, to the months that he spent buried in the hard end of the story and to the trust he built up with his subjects through the long nights they spent together in the darkness of the Sarajevo winter. He is a photographer who lives with people and becomes a part of their lives.

I recognize the worn look on the face of the man standing at his door with wood, his arm crooked defensively. I saw it so many times in Sarajevo as the winter months of 1992 dragged on into the new year. People's bodies were shrinking from the inside, recoiling from death, fear, hunger and cold. As a journalist, I never managed to describe that shrinking away, but Thomas Kern's pictures do.

The open-mouthed mother with her hair gently blow-dried and her neat black leather gloves should be promenading along the smart cobbled streets of the old Sarajevo. Instead she is watching her neighbours tearing each other apart for bits of wood. She looks straight into Thomas Kern's camera as if to ask: 'What is happening to all of us?'

The Red Cross say the refugees are . . . 'Refugee' is now a dead word. But looking at Kern's pictures of the old couple on their blanket, the man with his cardboard box, reminds me of all the school halls, factory floors and sheds where the refugees spread out their lives on the floor. In Zenica I remember an old woman building a shelf with a plank and two empty jam tins. In the corner of the rancid school gym she was trying to recreate the kitchen which she had lived in and had never expected to leave, the kitchen of the home that someone for some reason came and burned down.

The picture of the pig and the soldiers at the crossroads is in some ways the most frightening. There is a lack of control about the scene: in a minute, one of the soldiers just might blow the pig's head off. Tomorrow, as humanity recedes a little further, it might be a woman who is prodded at the crossroads. I remember one soldier describing how he raped a woman on the kerb. And how afterwards her mother and sister found her and pulled down the shreds of the woman's dress to make her decent. The pig at the crossroads is a warning.

As I was writing this introduction Thomas Kern rang. We talked about his pictures. He says they are about despair. His favourite is the boy holding the camera, his eyes asking: what am I doing here? Kern's achievement is to have captured this despair, and the confusion of ordinary people forced to live and love and die in the middle of a battlefield.

Maggie O'Kane

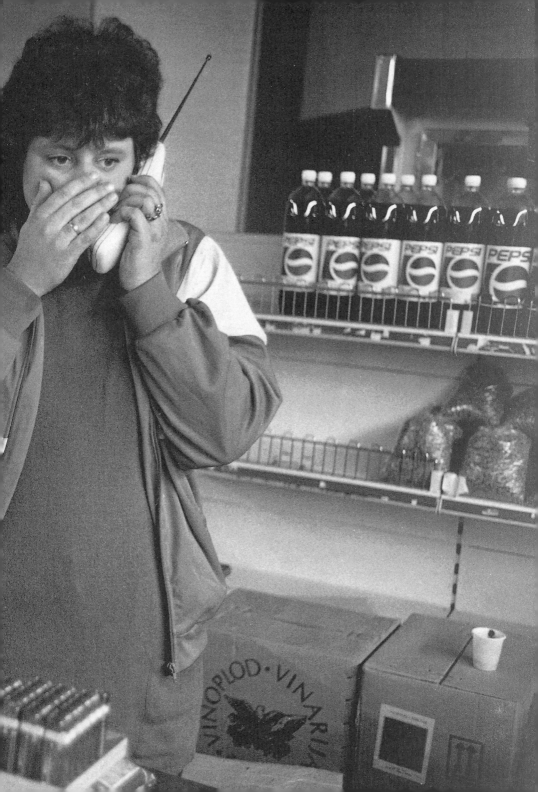

AMITAV GHOSH
DANCING IN CAMBODIA

On 10 May 1906, at two in the afternoon, a French liner called the *Amiral-Kersaint* set off from Saigon carrying a troupe of nearly a hundred classical dancers and musicians from the royal palace at Phnom Penh. The ship was bound for Marseille, where the dancers were to perform at a great colonial exhibition. It would be the first time Cambodian classical dance was performed in Europe.

Also travelling on the *Amiral-Kersaint* was the sixty-six-year-old ruler of Cambodia, King Sisowath, along with his entourage of several dozen princes, courtiers and officials. The King, who had been crowned two years before, had often spoken of his desire to visit France, and for him the voyage was the fulfilment of a lifelong dream.

The *Amiral-Kersaint* docked in Marseille on the morning of 11 June. The port was packed with curious onlookers; the city's trams had been busy since seven, transporting people to the vast, covered quay where the King and his entourage were to be received. The crowd was so large that two brigades of gendarmes and a detachment of mounted police had to be deployed to hold it back.

The crowd had its first, brief glimpse of the dancers when the *Amiral-Kersaint* loomed out of the fog shortly after nine and drew alongside the quay. A number of young women were spotted on the bridge and on the upper decks, flitting between portholes and clutching each other in what appeared to be surprise and astonishment.

Within minutes a gangplank decorated with tricoloured bunting had been thrown up to the ship. Soon the King himself appeared on deck, a good-humoured, smiling man, dressed in a tailcoat, a jewel-encrusted felt hat and a dhoti-like Cambodian *sampot* made of black silk. The King seemed alert, even jaunty, to those privileged to observe him at close range: a man of medium height, he had large, expressive eyes and a heavy-lipped mouth, topped by a thin moustache.

King Sisowath walked down the gangplank with three pages following close behind him; one bore a ceremonial gold cigarette

Opposite: A dancer of the Imperial Ballet in the courtyard of the school of classical dance in Phnom Penh, 1910.

case, another a gold lamp with a lighted wick, and a third a gold spittoon in the shape of an open lotus. The King was an instant favourite with the Marseillais crowd. The port resounded with claps and cheers as he was driven away in a ceremonial landau; he was applauded all the way to his specially-appointed apartments at the city's Préfecture.

In the meanwhile, within minutes of the King's departure from the port, a section of the crowd had rushed up the gangplank of the *Amiral-Kersaint* to see the dancers at first hand. For weeks now the Marseille newspapers had been full of tantalizing snippets of information: it was said that the dancers entered the palace as children and spent their lives in seclusion ever afterwards; that their lives revolved entirely around the royal family; that several were the King's mistresses and had even borne him children; that some of them had never stepped out of the palace grounds until this trip to France. European travellers went to great lengths to procure invitations to see these fabulous recluses performing in the palace at Phnom Penh: now here they were, in Marseille, visiting Europe for the very first time.

The dancers were on the ship's first-class deck; they seemed to be everywhere, running about, hopping, skipping, playing excitedly, feet skimming across the polished wood. The whole deck was a blur of legs, girls' legs, women's legs, 'fine, elegant legs,' for all the dancers were dressed in colourful *sampots* which ended shortly below the knee.

The onlookers were taken by surprise. They had expected perhaps a troupe of heavily-veiled, voluptuous Salomés; they were not quite prepared for the lithe, athletic women they encountered on the *Amiral-Kersaint*; nor, indeed, was the rest of Europe. An observer wrote later: 'With their hard and close-cropped hair, their figures like those of striplings, their thin, muscular legs like those of young boys, their arms and hands like those of little girls, they seem to belong to no definite sex. They have something of the child about them, something of the young warrior of antiquity and something of the woman.'

Sitting regally among the dancers, alternately stern and indulgent, affectionate and severe, was the slight fine-boned figure of the King's eldest daughter, Princess Soumphady. Dressed in a gold-brown *sampot* and a tunic of mauve silk, this redoubtable woman had an electrifying effect on the Marseillais crowd. They drank in every aspect of her appearance: her betel-stained teeth, her chestful of medals, her gold-embroidered shoes, her diamond brooches and her black silk stockings. Her manner, remarked one journalist, was at once haughty and childlike, her gaze direct and good-natured; she was amused by everything and nothing; she crossed her legs and clasped her shins just like a man: indeed, except for her dress she was very much like one man in particular —the romantic and whimsical Duke of Reichstadt, l'*Aiglon*, Napoleon's tubercular son.

Suddenly to the crowd's delight, the Princess's composure dissolved. A group of local women appeared on deck, accompanied by a ten-year-old boy, and along with all the other dancers, the Princess rushed over, admiring their clothes and exclaiming over the little boy.

The journalists were quick to seize this opportunity. 'Do you like French women?' they asked the Princess.

'Oh! Pretty, so pretty . . . ' she replied.

'And their clothes, their hats?'

'Just as pretty as they are themselves.'

'Would Your Highness like to wear clothes like those?'

'No!' the Princess said after a moment's reflection. 'No! I am not used to them and perhaps would not know how to wear them. But they are still pretty . . . oh! Yes . . . '

And with that she sank into what seemed to be an attitude of sombre and melancholy longing.

2

The only person I ever met who knew both Princess Soumphady and King Sisowath was a dancer named Chea Samy. She was said to be one of the Cambodia's greatest dancers, a national treasure. She was also Pol Pot's sister-in-law.

She was first pointed out to me at the School of Fine Arts in Phnom Penh—a rambling complex of buildings not far from the the Wat Phnom where the United Nation's twenty-thousand-strong peacekeeping force has its headquarters. It was January, only four months before coutry-wide elections were to be held under the auspices of Untac, as the UN's Transitional Authority in Cambodia is universally known. Phnom Penh had temporarily become one of the most cosmopolitan towns in the world, its streets a traffic nightmare, with Untac's white Land Cruisers cutting through shoals of careering scooters, mopeds and *cyclopousses*, like whales cruising through drifting plankton.

The School of Fine Arts was hidden from this multinational traffic by piles of uncleared refuse and a string of shacks and shanties. Its walled compound was oddly self-contained and its cavernous halls and half-finished classrooms were filled with the self-sustaining, honeycomb bustle of a huge television studio.

I had only recently arrived in Phnom Penh when I first met Chea Samy. She was sitting on a bench in the school's vast training hall: a small woman with the kind of poise that goes with the confidence of great beauty. She was dressed in an ankle-length skirt, and her grey hair was cut short. She was presiding over a class of about forty boys and girls, watching them go through their exercises, her gentle, rounded face tense with concentration. Occasionally she would spring off the bench and bend back a dancer's arm or push in a waist, working as a sculptor does, by touch, moulding their limbs like clay.

At the time I had no idea whether Chea Samy had known Princess Soumphady or not. I had become curious about the Princess and her father, King Sisowath, after learning of their journey to Europe in 1906, and I wanted to know more about them.

Chea Samy's eyes widened when I asked her about Princess Soumphady at the end of her class. She looked from me to the student who was interpreting for us as though she couldn't quite believe she had heard the name right. I reassured her: yes, I really did mean Princess Soumphady, Princess Sisowath Soumphady.

She smiled in the indulgent, misty way in which people recall a favourite aunt. Yes, of course she had known Princess Soumphady, she said. As a little girl, when she first went into the Palace to learn dance, it was Princess Soumphady who had been in charge of the dancers: for a while the Princess had brought her up . . .

The second time I met Chea Samy was at her house. She lives

a few miles from Pochentong airport, on Phnom Penh's rapidly-expanding frontier, in an area that is largely farm land, with a few houses strung along a dirt road. The friend whom I had persuaded to come along with me to translate took an immediate dislike to the place. It was already late afternoon, and she did not relish the thought of driving back through those roads in the dark.

My friend, Molyka, was a mid-level civil servant, a poised, attractive woman in her early thirties, painfully soft-spoken, in the Khmer way. She had spent a short while studying in Australia on a government scholarship, and spoke English with a better feeling for nuance and idiom than any of the professional interpreters I had met. If I was to visit Chea Samy, I had decided, it would be with her. But Molyka proved hard to persuade: she had become frightened of venturing out of the centre of the city.

Not long ago she had been out driving with a friend of hers, the wife of an Untac official, when her car was stopped at a busy roundabout by a couple of soldiers. They were wearing the uniform of the 'State of Cambodia', the faction that currently governs most of the country. 'I work for the government too,' she told them, 'in an important ministry.' They ignored her; they wanted money. She didn't have much, only a couple of thousand riels. They asked for cigarettes; she didn't have any. They told her to get out of the car and accompany them into a building. They were about to take her away when her friend interceded. They let her go eventually: they left UN people alone on the whole. But as she drove away they had shouted after her: 'We're going to be looking out for you: you won't always have an Untac in the car.'

Molyka was scared, and she had reason to be. The government's underpaid (often unpaid) soldiers and policemen were increasingly given to banditry and bouts of inexplicable violence. Not long before, I had gone to visit a hospital in an area where there were frequent hostilities between State troops and the Khmer Rouge. I had expected that the patients in the casualty ward would be principally victims of mines and Khmer Rouge shell-fire. Instead I found a group of half a dozen women, some with children, lying on grimy mats, their faces and bodies pitted and torn with black

Overleaf: A pavement barbershop in Phnom Penh.

Photo: Patrick Zachmann (Magnum)

shrapnel wounds. They had been travelling in a pick-up truck to sell vegetables at a nearby market when they were stopped by a couple of State soldiers. The soldiers asked for money; the women handed out some but the soldiers wanted more. The women had no more to give and told them so. The soldiers let the truck pass but stopped it again that evening, on its way back. They didn't ask for anything this time; they simply detonated a fragmentation mine.

A couple of weeks after that visit I was travelling in a taxi with four Cambodians along a dusty, potholed road in a sparsely inhabited region in the north-west of the country. I had dozed off in the front seat when I was woken by the rattle of gunfire. I looked up and saw a State soldier standing in the middle of the dirt road, directly ahead. He was in his teens, like most uniformed Cambodians; he was wearing round, wire-rimmed sun-glasses and his pelvis was thrust out, MTV-style. But instead of a guitar he had an AK-47 in his hands and he was spraying the ground in front of us with bullets, creating a delicate tracery of dust.

The taxi jolted to a halt; the driver thrust an arm out of the window and waved his wallet. The soldier did not seem to notice; he was grinning and swaying, probably drunk. When I sat up in the front seat, the barrel of his gun rose slowly until it was pointing directly at my forehead. Looking into the unblinking eye of that AK-47, two slogans unaccountably flashed through my mind; they were scrawled all over the walls of Calcutta when I was the same age as that soldier. One was, 'Power comes from the barrel of a gun' and the other, 'You can't make an omelette without breaking eggs.' It turned out he only had the first in mind.

Molyka had heard stories like these, but living in Phnom Penh, working as a civil servant, she had been relatively sheltered until that day when her car was stopped. The incident frightened her in ways she couldn't quite articulate; it reawakened a host of long-dormant fears. Molyka was only thirteen in 1975, when the Khmer Rouge took Phnom Penh. She was evacuated with her whole extended family, fourteen people in all, to a labour camp in the province of Kompong Thom. A few months later she was separated from the others and sent to work in a fishing village on Cambodia's immense freshwater lake, the Tonlé Sap. For the next three years she worked as a servant and nursemaid for a family of fisherfolk.

She only saw her parents once in that time. One day she was sent to a village near Kompong Thom with a group of girls. While sitting by the roadside she happened to look up from her basket of fish and saw her mother walking towards her. Her first instinct was to turn away; every detail matched those of her most frequently recurring dream: the parched countryside, the ragged palms, her mother coming out of the red dust of the road, walking straight towards her. . .

She didn't see her mother again until 1979, when she came back to Phnom Penh after the Vietnamese invasion. She managed to locate her as well as two of her brothers after months of searching. Of the fourteen people who had walked out of her house three and a half years before, ten were dead, including her father, two brothers and a sister. Her mother had become an abject, terrified creature after her father was called away into the fields one night, never to return. One of her brothers was too young to work; the other had willed himself into a state of guilt-stricken paralysis after revealing their father's identity to the Khmer Rouge in a moment of inattention—he now held himself responsible for his father's death.

Their family was from the social group that was hardest hit by the revolution: the urban middle classes. City people by definition, they were herded into rural work camps; the institutions and forms of knowledge that sustained them were destroyed—the judicial system was dismantled, the practice of formal medicine was discontinued; schools and colleges were shut down; banks and credit were done away with; indeed the very institution of money was abolished. Cambodia's was not a civil war in the same sense as Somalia's or the former Yugoslavia's, fought over the fetishism of small differences: it was a war on history itself, an experiment in the reinvention of society. No regime in history had ever before made so systematic and sustained an attack on the middle class. Yet, if the experiment was proof of anything at all, it was ultimately of the indestructibility of the middle class, of its extraordinary tenacity and resilience; its capacity to preserve its forms of knowledge and expression through the most extreme kinds of adversity.

Molyka was only seventeen then but she was the one who had to cope because no one else in the family could. She took a job in the army and put herself and her brothers through school and college; later she acquired a house and a car; she adopted a child and—like so many people in Phnom Penh—she took in and supported about half a dozen complete strangers. In one way or another she was responsible for supporting a dozen lives.

Yet now Molyka, who at the age of thirty-one had already lived through several lifetimes, was afraid of driving into the outskirts of the city. Over the last year the edges of the life she had put together were beginning to look frayed. Paradoxically, at precisely the moment when the world had ordained peace and democracy for Cambodia, uncertainty had reached its peak within the country. Nobody knew who would come to power after the UN-sponsored elections, or what would happen when they did. Her colleagues had all become desperate to make some provision for the future—by buying, stealing, selling whatever was at hand. Those two soldiers who had stopped her car were no exception. Everyone she knew was a little like that now—ministers, bureaucrats, policemen: they were all people who saw themselves faced with yet another beginning.

Now Molyka was driving out to meet Pol Pot's brother and sister-in-law: relatives of a man whose name was indelibly associated with the deaths of her own father and nine other members of her family. She had gasped in disbelief when I first asked her to accompany me: to her, as to most people in Cambodia, the name 'Pol Pot' was an abstraction; it referred to a time, an organization, a form of terror—it was almost impossible to associate it with a mere human being, one that had brothers, relatives, sisters-in-law. But she was curious too, and in the end, overcoming her fear of the neighbourhood, she drove me out in her own car, into the newly-colonized farmland near Pochentong airport.

The house, when we found it, proved to be a comfortable wooden structure, built in the traditional Khmer style, with its details picked out in bright blue. Like all such houses it was supported on stilts, and as we walked in, a figure detached itself from the shadows beneath the house and came towards us: a tall, vigorous-looking man dressed in a sarong. He had a broad, pleasant face and short, spiky grey hair. The resemblance to Pol Pot was startling.

I glanced at Molyka: she bowed, joining her hands, as he welcomed us in, and they exchanged a few friendly words of greeting. His wife was waiting upstairs, he said, and led us up a wooden staircase to a large, airy room with a few photographs on the bare walls: portraits of relatives and ancestors, of the kind that hang in every Khmer house. Chea Samy was sitting on a couch at the far end of the room: she waved us in and her husband took his leave of us, smiling, hands folded.

'I wanted to attack him when I first saw him,' Molyka told me later. 'But then I thought—it's not his fault. What has he ever done to me?'

3

Chea Samy was taken into the palace in Phnom Penh in 1925, as a child of six, to begin her training in classical dance. She was chosen after an audition in which thousands of children participated. Her parents were delighted: dance was one of the few means by which a commoner could gain entry into the palace in those days, and to have a child accepted often meant preferment for the whole family.

King Sisowath was in his eighties when she went into palace. He had spent most of his life waiting in the wings, wearing the pinched footwear of a Crown Prince while his half-brother Norodom ruled centre-stage. The two princes held dramatically different political views: Norodom was bitterly opposed to the French, while Sisowath was a passionate Francophile. It was because of French support that Sisowath was eventually able to succeed to the throne, in preference to his half-brother's innumerable sons.

Something of an eccentric all his life, King Sisowath kept no fixed hours and spent a good deal of his time smoking opium with his sons and advisers. During his visit to France the authorities even improvised a small opium den in his apartments at the Préfecture in Marseille. '*Voila!*' cried the newspapers, 'An opium den in the Préfecture! There's no justice left!' But it was the French who kept the King supplied with opium in Cambodia, and they could hardly do otherwise when he was a state guest in France.

By the time Chea Samy entered the palace in 1925 King Sisowath's behaviour had become erratic in the extreme. He would wander nearly naked around the grounds of the palace wearing nothing but a *kramar*, a length of checkered cloth, knotted loosely around his waist. It was Princess Soumphady who was the central figure in the lives of the children of the dance troupe: she was a surrogate mother who tempered the rigours of their training with a good deal of kindly indulgence, making sure they were well fed and clothed.

On King Sisowath's death in 1927, his son Monivong succeeded to the throne, and soon the regime in the palace underwent a change. The new King's favourite mistress was a talented dancer called Luk Khun Meak, and she now gradually took over Princess Soumphady's role as 'the lady in charge of the women.' Luk Khun Meak made use of her influence to introduce several members of her family into the palace. Among them were a few relatives from a small village in the province of Kompong Thom. One—later to become Chea Samy's husband—was given a job as a clerk at the palace. He in turn brought two of his brothers with him, so they could go to school in Phnom Penh. The youngest of the two was a boy of six called Saloth Sar—it was he who was later to take the *nom de guerre*, Pol Pot.

Chea Samy made a respectful gesture at a picture on the wall behind her, and I looked up to find myself transfixed by Luk Khun Meak's stern, frowning gaze. 'She was killed by Pol Pot,' said Chea Samy, using the generic phrase with which Cambodians refer to the deaths of that time. The distinguished old dancer, mistress of King Monivong, died of starvation after the revolution. One of her daughters was apprehended by the Khmer Rouge while trying to buy rice with a little bit of gold. Her breasts were sliced off, and she was left to bleed to death.

'What was Pol Pot like as a boy?' I asked, inevitably.

Chea Samy hesitated for a moment: it was easy to see that she had often been asked the question before and had thought about it at some length. 'He was a very good boy,' she said at last, emphatically. 'In all the years he lived with me, he never gave me any trouble at all.'

Then, with a despairing gesture, she said, 'I have been

married to his brother for fifty years now, and I can tell you that my husband is a good man, a kind man. He doesn't drink, doesn't smoke, has never made trouble between friends, never hit his nephews, never made difficulties for his children . . . '

She gave up; her hands flipped over in a flutter of bewilderment and fell limp into her lap.

The young Saloth Sar's palace connection ensured places for him at some of the country's better-known schools. In 1949 he was awarded a scholarship to study electronics in Paris. When he returned to Cambodia, three years later, he began working in secret for the Indochina Communist Party. Neither Chea Samy nor her husband saw much of him, and he told them very little of what he was doing. Then in 1963 he disappeared; they learned later that he had fled into the jungle along with several well-known leftists and Communists. That was the last they heard of Saloth Sar.

In 1975 when the Khmer Rouge seized power, Chea Samy and her husband were evacuated like everyone else. They were sent off to a village of 'old people', long-time Khmer Rouge sympathizers and, along with all the other 'new people', were made to work in the rice fields. For the next couple of years there was a complete news blackout, and they knew nothing of what had happened: it was a part of the Khmer Rouge's mechanics of terror to deprive the population of knowledge. They first began to hear the words 'Pol Pot' in 1978 when the regime tried to create a personality cult around its leader in an attempt to stave off imminent collapse.

Chea Samy was working in a communal kitchen at the time, cooking and washing dishes. Late that year some party workers stuck a poster on the walls of the kitchen: they said it was a picture of their leader, Pol Pot. She knew who it was the moment she set eyes on the picture.

That was how she discovered that the leader of Angkar, the terrifying, inscrutable 'Organization,' that ruled over their lives, was none other than little Saloth Sar.

4

A few months later, in January 1979, the Vietnamese 'broke' Cambodia—as the Khmer phrase has it—and the regime collapsed. Shortly afterwards Chea Samy and her husband, like all the other evacuees, began to drift out of the villages in which they had been imprisoned. Carrying nothing but a few cupfuls of dry rice, barefoot, half-starved and dressed in rags, they began to find their way back towards the places they had once known, where they had once had friends and relatives.

Walking down the dusty country roads, encountering others like themselves, the bands of 'new people' slowly began to rediscover the exhilaration of speech. For more than three years now they had not been able to speak freely to anyone with confidence, not even their own children. Many had reinvented their lives in order to protect themselves from the obsessive biographical curiosity of Angkar's cadres. Now, talking on the roads, they slowly began to shed their assumed personae; they began to mine their memories for information about the people they had met and heard of over the last few years, the names of the living and the dead.

It was the strangest of times.

The American Quaker, Eva Mysliwiec, arrived in the country in 1980; she was one of the first foreign relief workers to come to Cambodia and is now a legend in Phnom Penh. Some of her most vivid memories of that period are of the volcanic outbursts of speech that erupted everywhere at unexpected moments. Friends and acquaintances would suddenly begin to describe what they had lived through and seen, what had happened to them and their families and how they had managed to survive. Often people would wake up looking drained and haggard; they would see things at night, in their dreams, all those things they had tried to put out of their minds when they were happening because they would have gone mad if they'd stopped to think about them—a brother called away in the dark; an infant battered against a tree; children starving to death. When you saw them in the morning

Opposite: Cambodian refugees attempting to reach the Thai border, November 1979.

Photo: Hulton Deutsch

and asked what had happened during the night, they would make a circular gesture, as though the past had been unfolding before them like a turning reel, and they would say, simply, 'Camera.'

Eventually, after weeks of wandering, Chea Samy and her husband reached the western outskirts of Phnom Penh. There, one day, entirely by accident, she ran into a girl who had studied dance with her before the revolution. The girl cried, 'Teacher! Where have you been? They've been looking for you everywhere.'

There was no real administration in those days. Many of the resistance leaders who had come back to Cambodia with the Vietnamese had never held administrative positions before: for the most part they were breakaway members of the Khmer Rouge who had been opposed to the policies of Pol Pot and his group. They had to learn on the job when they returned, and for a long time there was nothing like a real government in Cambodia. The country was like a shattered slate: before you could think of drawing lines on it, you had to find the pieces and fit them together.

But already the fledgling Ministry of Culture had launched an effort to locate the classical dancers and teachers who had survived. Its officials were overjoyed to find Chea Samy. They quickly arranged for her to travel through the country to look for other teachers and for young people with talent and potential.

'It was very difficult,' said Chea Samy. 'I did not know where to go, where to start. Most of the teachers had been killed or maimed, and the others were in no state to begin teaching again. Anyway there was no one to teach: so many of the children were orphans, half-starved. They had no idea of dance; they had never seen Khmer dance. It seemed impossible; there was no place to begin.'

Her voice was quiet and matter of fact but there was a quality of muted exhilaration in it too. I recognized that note at once for I had heard it before: in Molyka's voice, for example, when she spoke of the first years after the 'Pol-Pot-time', when slowly, patiently, she had picked through the rubble around her, building a life for herself and her family. I was to hear it again and again in Cambodia—most often in the voices of women. They had lived through an experience very nearly unique in human history: they had found themselves adrift in the ruins of a society which had collapsed into a formless heap, its scaffolding systematically dismantled, picked apart with the tools of a murderously rational form of social science. At a time when there was widespread fear and uncertainty about the intentions of the Vietnamese, they had had to start from the beginning, literally, like rag-pickers, piecing their families, their homes, their lives together from the little that was left.

Like everyone around her, Chea Samy too had started all over again—at the age of sixty, with her health shattered by the years of famine and hard labour. Working with quiet, dogged persistence, she and a handful of other dancers and musicians slowly brought together a ragged, half-starved bunch of orphans and castaways, and with the discipline of their long, rigorous years of training they began to resurrect the art that Princess Soumphady and Luk Khun Meak had passed on to them in that long-ago world when King Sisowath reigned. Out of the ruins around them they began to forge the means of denying Pol Pot his victory.

5

Everywhere he went on his tour of France, King Sisowath was accompanied by his Palace Minister, an official who bore the simple name of Thiounn (pronounced *Choun*). For all his Francophilia, King Sisowath spoke no French, and it was Minister Thiounn who served as his interpreter.

Minister Thiounn was widely acknowledged to be one of the most remarkable men in Cambodia: his career was without precedent in the aristocratic, rigidly hierarchical world of Cambodian officialdom. Starting as an interpreter for the French at the age of nineteen, he had overcome the twin disadvantages of modest birth and a mixed Khmer-Vietnamese ancestry to become the most powerful official at the court of Phnom Penh: the Minister, simultaneously, of Finance, Fine Arts and Palace Affairs.

This spectacular rise owed a great deal to the French, to whom he had been of considerable assistance in their decades-long struggle with Cambodia's ruling family. His role had earned him the bitter contempt of certain members of the royal family, and a famous prince had even denounced the 'boy-interpreter' as a French collaborator. But with French dominance in Cambodia already assured, there was little that any Cambodian prince could do to check the growing influence of Minister Thiounn. Norodom Sihanouk, King Sisowath's great-grandson, spent several of his early years on the throne smarting under Minister Thiounn's tutelage: he was to describe him later as a 'veritable little king . . . as powerful as the French *Résidents-Supérieurs* of the period.'

The trip to France was to become something of a personal triumph for Minister Thiounn, earning him compliments from a number of French ministers and politicians. But it also served a more practical function, for travelling on the *Amiral-Kersaint*, along with the dancers and the rest of the royal entourage, was the Minister's son, Thiounn Hol. In the course of his stay in France the Minister succeeded in entering him as a student in the École Coloniale. He was the only Cambodian commoner to be accepted: the three other Cambodians who were admitted at the same time were all members of the royal family.

Not unpredictably the Minister's son proved to be a far better student than the princelings and went on to become the first Cambodian to earn university qualifications in France. Later, the Minister's grandsons, scions of what was by then the second most powerful family in Cambodia, were to make the same journey out to France.

One of those grandsons, Thiounn Mumm acquired a doctorate in applied science and became the first Cambodian to graduate from the exalted École Polytechnique. In the process he also became a central figure within the small circle of Cambodians in France: the story goes that he made a point of befriending every student from his country and even went to the airport to receive newcomers.

Thiounn Mumm was, in other words, part mentor, part older brother and part leader: a figure immediately recognizable to anyone who has ever inhabited the turbulent limbo of the Asian or African student in Europe—that curious circumstance of social dislocation and emotional turmoil that for more than a century now has provided the site for some of the globe's most explosive political encounters. And Thiounn Mumm was no ordinary student mentor for he was also a member of a political dynasty—the Cambodian equivalent of the Nehrus or the Bhuttos.

Among Thiounn Mumm's many protégés was the young Pol Pot, then still known as Saloth Sar. It is generally believed that it was Thiounn Mumm who was responsible for his induction into the French Communist Party in 1952. Those Parisian loyalties have proved unshakeable: Thiounn Mumm and two of his brothers have been members of Pol Pot's innermost clique ever since.

That this ultra-radical clique should be so intimately linked with the palace and with colonial officialdom is not particularly a matter of surprise in Cambodia. 'Revolutions and *coups d'état* always start in the courtyards of the palace,' a well-known political figure in Phnom Penh told me. 'It's the people within who realize that the King is ordinary, while everyone else takes him for a god.'

In this case, the proximity of the Thiounns and Pol Pot to the élitist, racially exclusive culture of the court may have had a formative influence on some aspects of their political vision: it may even have been responsible, as the historian Ben Kiernan has suggested, for the powerful strain of 'national and racial grandiosity' in the ideology of their clique. That strain has eventually proved dominant: the Khmer Rouge's programme now consists largely of an undisguisedly racist nationalism, whose principal targets, for the time being, are Vietnam and Cambodia's own Vietnamese minority.

A recent defector, describing his political training with the Khmer Rouge, told UN officials that: 'As far as the Vietnamese are concerned, whenever we meet them we must kill them, whether they are militaries or civilians, because they are not ordinary civilians but soldiers disguised as civilians. We must kill them, whether they are men, women or children, there is no distinction, they are enemies. Children are not militaries but if they are born or grow up in Cambodia, when they will be adult, they will consider Cambodian land as theirs. So we make no distinction. As to women, they give birth to Vietnamese children.'

Shortly before the elections, in a sudden enlargement of its racist vocabulary, the Khmer Rouge also began to incite violence against 'white-skinned, point-nosed Untac soldiers.'

6

The more I learned of Pol Pot's journey to France, and of the other journeys that had preceded it, the more curious I became about his origins. One day, late in January, I decided to go looking for his ancestral village in the province of Kompong Thom.

Kompong Thom has great military importance, for it straddles the vital middle section of Cambodia, the strategic heart of the country. The town of Kompong Thom is very small: a string of houses that grows suddenly into a bullet-riddled market-place, a school, a hospital, a few roads that extend all of a hundred yards, a bridge across the Sen river, a tall, freshly-painted Wat, a few outcrops of blue-signposted Untac-land and then, the countryside again, flat and dusty, clumps of palms leaning raggedly over the earth, fading into the horizon in a dull grey-green patina, like mould upon a copper tray.

Two of the country's most important roadways intersect to the north of the little town. One leads directly to Thailand and the Khmer rouge controls large chunks of territory on either side of it. This road is one of the most hotly contested in Cambodia and there are daily exchanges of shells and gunfire between Khmer Rouge guerrillas and the State of Cambodia troops who are posted along it.

The point where the two roads meet is guarded by an old army encampment, now controlled by the State. Its perimeter is heavily mined: the mines are reputed to have been laid by the State itself—partly to keep the Khmer Rouge out, but also to keep its own none-too-willing soldiers in.

Here, in this strategic hub, this centre of centres, looking for Pol Pot's ancestral home, inevitably I came across someone from mine. He was a Bangladeshi sergeant, a large, friendly man with a bushy moustache: we had an ancestral district in common, in Bangladesh, and the unexpectedness of this discovery—at the edge of a Cambodian minefield—linked us immediately in a ridiculously intimate kind of bonhomie.

The sergeant and his colleagues were teaching a group of Cambodian soldiers professional de-mining techniques. They were themselves trained sappers and engineers, but as it happened none of them had ever seen or worked in a minefield that had been laid with intent to kill, so to speak. For their Cambodian charges, on the other hand, mines were a hazard of everyday life, like snakes or spiders.

This irony was not lost on the Bangladeshi sergeant. 'They think nothing of laying mines,' he said, in trenchant Bengali. 'They scatter them about like popped rice. Often they mine their own doorstep before going to bed, to keep thieves out. They mine their cars, their television sets, even their vegetable patches. They don't care who gets killed; life really has no value here.'

He shook his head in perplexity, looking at his young Cambodian charges: they were working in teams of two on the minefield—an expanse of scrub and grass that had been divided into narrow strips with tape. The teams were inching along their strips, one man scanning the ground ahead with a mine-detector, the other lying flat, armed with a probe and trowel, ready to dig for mines. By this slow, painstaking method, the team had cleared a couple of acres in a month. This was considered good progress, and the sergeant had reason to be pleased with the job he and his unit had done.

In the course of their work, the sergeant and his colleagues had become friends with several Cambodian members of their team. But the better they got to know them and the better they liked them, the more feckless they seemed and the more hopeless the country's situation. This despite the fact that Cambodians in general have a standard of living that would be considered enviable by most people in Bangladesh or India; despite the fact that Kompong Thom—for all that it has been on the front line for decades—is better-ordered than any provincial town in the subcontinent; and despite the fact that the sergeant was himself from a country that had suffered the ravages of a bloody civil war in the early seventies.

'They're working hard here because they're getting paid in dollars,' the sergeant said. 'For them it's all dollars, dollars, dollars. Sometimes, at the end of the day, we have to hand out a couple of dollars from our own pockets to get them to finish the day's work.'

He laughed. 'It's their own country, and we have to pay them

to make it safe. What I wonder is: what will they do when we're gone?'

I told him what a long-time foreign resident of Phnom Penh had said to me: that Cambodia was actually only fifteen years old; that it had managed remarkably well considering it had been built up almost from scratch after the fall of the Pol Pot regime in 1979; and that this had been achieved in a situation of near-complete international isolation. Europe and Japan had received massive amounts of aid after the Second World War, but Cambodia, which had been subjected to one of the heaviest bombings in the history of war, had got virtually nothing. Yet Cambodians had made do with what they had.

But the sergeant was looking for large-scale proofs of progress—roads, a functioning postal system, Projects, Schemes, Plans—and their lack rendered meaningless those tiny, cumulative efforts by which individuals and families reclaim their lives—a shutter repaired, a class taught, a palm-tree tended—which are no longer noticeable once they are done since they sink into the order of normalcy, where they belong, and cease to be acts of affirmation and hope. He was the smallest of cogs in the vast machinery of the UN, but, no less than the international bureaucrats and experts in Phnom Penh, his vision of the country was organized around his part in saving it from itself.

'What Cambodians are good at is destruction,' he said. 'They know nothing about building—about putting things up and carrying on.'

He waved good-naturedly at the Cambodians, and they waved back, bobbing their heads, smiling and bowing. Both sides were working hard at their jobs, the expert and the amateur, the feckless and the responsible: doughty rescuer and hapless rescued were both taking their jobs equally seriously.

Opposite: A resident of a rehabilitation centre for the handicapped in Phnom Penh, where victims of land-mines assist in making their own artificial limbs.

7

I got blank stares when I asked where Pol Pot's village was. Pol Pot had villages on either side of Route 12, people said, dozens of them, nobody could get to them, they were in the forest, surrounded by minefields. I might as well have asked where the State of Cambodia was. Nor did it help to ask about 'Saloth Sar': nobody seemed ever to have heard of that name.

One of the people I asked, a young Cambodian called Sros, offered to help, although he was just as puzzled by the question as everybody else. He worked for a relief agency and had spent a lot of time in Kompong Thom. He had never heard anybody mention Pol Pot's village and would have been sceptical if he had. But I persuaded him that Pol Pot was really called Saloth Sar and had been born near the town: I'd forgotten the name of the village, but I had seen it mentioned in books and knew it was close by.

He was intrigued. He borrowed a scooter, and we drove down the main street in Kompong Thom, stopping passers-by and asking respectfully: 'Bong, do you know where Pol Pot's village is?'

They looked at us in disbelief and hurried away: either they didn't know or they weren't saying. Then Sros stopped to ask a local district official, a bowed, earnest-looking man with a twitch that ran all the way down the right side of his face. The moment I saw him, I was sure he would know. He did. He lowered his voice and whispered quickly into Sros's ear: the village was called Sbauv, and to get to it we had to go past the hospital and follow the dirt road along the River Sen. He stopped to look over his shoulder and pointed down the road.

There was perhaps an hour of sunlight left, and it wasn't safe to be out after dark. But Sros was undeterred; the thought that we were near Pol Pot's birthplace had a galvanic effect on him. He was determined to get there as soon as possible.

Sros had spent almost his entire adult life behind barbed wire, one and a half miles of it, in a refugee camp on the Thai border. He had entered it at the age of thirteen and had come to manhood circling around and around the perimeter, month after month, year after year, waiting to see who got out, who got a visa, who went mad, who got raped, who got shot by the Thai guards. He was twenty-five now, diminutive but wiry, very slight of build. He had converted to Christianity at the camp, and there was an earnestness behind his ready smile and easy-going manners that hinted at a deeply-felt piety.

Sros was too young to recall much of the 'Pol-Pot-time', but he remembered vividly his journey to the Thai border with his parents. They left in 1982, three years after the Vietnamese invasion. Things were hard where they were, and they'd heard from Western radio broadcasts that there were camps on the border where they would be looked after and fed.

Things hadn't turned out quite as they had imagined: they ended up in a camp run by a conservative Cambodian political faction, a kind of living hell. But they bribed a 'guide' to get them across to a UN-run camp, Khao I Dang, where the conditions were better. Sros went to school and learned English and after years of waiting, fruitlessly, for a visa to the West, he took the plunge and crossed over into Cambodia. That was a year ago. With his education and his knowledge of English he had found a job without difficulty, but he was still keeping his name on the rosters of the UN High Commission for Refugees.

'My father says to me, there will be peace in your lifetime and you will be happy,' he told me. 'My grandfather used to tell my father the same thing, and now I say the same thing to my nephews and nieces. It's always the same.'

We left Kompong Thom behind almost before we knew it. A dirt road snaked away from the edge of the city, shaded by trees and clumps of bamboo. The road was an estuary of deep red dust: the wheels of the ox-carts that came rumbling towards us churned up crimson waves that billowed outwards and up into the sky. The dust hung above the road far into the distance, like spray above a rocky coastline, glowing red in the sunset.

Flanking the road on one side were shanties and small dwellings, the poorest I had yet seen in Cambodia: some of them no more than frames stuck into the ground and covered with plaited palm leaves. Even the larger houses seemed little more than shanties on stilts. On the other side of the road the ground dropped away sharply to the River Sen: a shrunken stream now, in the dry season, flowing sluggishly along at the bottom of its steep-sided channel.

It was impossible to tell where one village ended and another began. We stopped to ask a couple of times, the last time at a stall where a woman was selling cigarettes and fruit. She pointed over her shoulder: one of Pol Pot's brothers lived in the house behind the stall, she said, and another in a palm-thatch shanty in the adjacent yard.

We drove into the yard and looked up at the house: it was large compared to those around it, a typical wooden Khmer house on stilts, with chickens roosting underneath and clothes drying between the pillars. It had clearly seen much better days and was badly in need of repairs.

The decaying house and the dilapidated, palm-thatched shanty in the yard took me by surprise. I remembered having read that Pol Pot's father was a well-to-do farmer and had expected something less humble. Sros was even more surprised: perhaps he had assumed that the relatives of politicians always got rich, one way or another. There was an augury of something unfamiliar here—a man of power who had done nothing to help his own kin. It was a reminder that we were confronting a phenomenon that was completely at odds with quotidian expectation.

Then an elderly woman with close-cropped white hair appeared on the veranda of the house. Sros said a few words to her and she immediately invited us up. Greeting us with folded hands, she asked us to seat ourselves on a mat while she went inside to find her husband. Like many Khmer dwellings the house was sparsely furnished, the walls bare except for a few religious pictures and images of the Buddha.

The woman returned followed by a tall gaunt man dressed in a faded sarong. He did not look as much like Pol Pot as the brother I had met briefly in Phnom Penh, but the resemblance was still unmistakeable.

His name was Loth Sieri, he said, seating himself beside us, and he was the second-oldest of the brothers. Saloth Sar had gone away to Phnom Penh while he was still quite young, and after that

Opposite: Pol Pot, pictured on his 'retirement' as commander of the Khmer Rouge in September 1979.

they had not seen very much of him. He had gone from school to college in Phnom Penh, and then finally to Paris. He smiled ruefully. 'It was the knowledge he got in Paris that made him what he is,' he said.

He had visited them a few times after returning to Cambodia but then he had disappeared and they had never seen him again: it was more than twenty years now since he, Loth Sieri, had set eyes on him. They had been treated no differently from anyone else during the Pol-Pot-time; they had not had the remotest idea that 'Pol Pot' was their brother Sar, born in their house. They only found out afterwards.

Was Saloth Sar born in this very house? I asked. Yes, they said, in the room beside us, right next to veranda.

When he came back from France, I asked, had he ever talked about his life in Paris—what he'd done, who his friends were, what the city was like?

At that moment, with cows lowing in the gathering darkness, the journey to Paris from that village on the Sen river seemed an extraordinary odyssey. I found myself very curious to know how he and his brothers had imagined Paris, and their own brother in it. But no. The old man shook his head: Saloth Sar had never talked about France after he came back. Maybe he had shown them some pictures—Loth Sieri couldn't recall.

I remembered, from David Chandler's biography, that Pol Pot was very well read as a young man, and knew large tracts of Rimbaud and Verlaine by heart. But I was not surprised to discover that he had never allowed his family the privilege of imagining.

Just before getting up, I asked if he remembered his relative, the dancer Luk Khun Meak, who had first introduced his family into the royal palace. He nodded and I asked, 'Did you ever see her dance?'

He smiled and shook his head; no, he had never seen any 'royal' dancing, except in pictures.

It was almost dark now; somewhere in the north, near the minefield, there was the sound of gunfire. We got up to go, and the whole family walked down with us. After I had said goodbye and was about to climb on to the scooter, Sros whispered in my ear that it might be a good idea to give the old man some money. I had not thought of it; I took some money out of my pocket and put it in his hands.

He made a gesture of acknowledgement, and as we were about to leave he said a few words to Sros.

'What did he say?' I asked Sros when we were back on the road.

Shouting above the wind, Sros said: 'He asked me: "Do you think there will be peace now?"'

'And what did you tell him?' I said.

'I told him, "I wish I could say yes."'

8

On 10 July 1906, one month after their arrival in France, the dancers performed at a reception given by the Minister of Colonies in the Bois du Boulogne in Paris. 'Never has there been a more brilliant Parisian fête,' said *Le Figaro*, 'nor one with such novel charm.' Invitations were much sought after, and on the night of the performance cars and illuminated carriages invaded the park like an 'army of fireflies.'

While the performance was in progress a correspondent spotted the most celebrated Parisian of all in the audience, the bearded Mosaic figure of 'the great Rodin [going] into ecstasies over the little virgins of Phnom Penh, whose immaterial silhouettes he drew with infinite love.'

Rodin, now at the age of sixty-six, France's acknowledged apostle of the arts, fell immediately captive: in Princess Soumphady's young charges he discovered the infancy of Europe. 'These Cambodians have shown us everything that antiquity could have contained,' he wrote soon afterwards. 'It is impossible to think of anyone wearing human nature to such perfection; except them and the Greeks.'

Two days after the performance Rodin presented himself at the dancers' Paris lodgings in the Avenue Malakoff with a sketchbook under his arm. The dancers were packing their belongings in preparation for their return to Marseille, but Rodin was admitted to the grounds of the mansion and given leave to do

Above: Rodin drawing a Cambodian dancer, Marseille, 1906.

what he pleased. He executed several celebrated sketches that day, including a few of King Sisowath.

By the end of the day the artist was so smitten with the dancers that he accompanied them to the station, bought a ticket and travelled to Marseille on the same train. He had packed neither clothes nor materials and, according to one account, upon arriving in Marseille and finding that he was out of paper, he had to buy brown paper bags from a grocery store.

Over the next few days, sketching feverishly in the gardens of the villa where the dancers were now lodged, Rodin seemed to lose thirty years. The effort involved in sketching his favourite models, three restless fourteen-year-olds called Sap, Soun and Yem, appeared to rejuvenate the artist. A French official saw him placing a sheet of white paper on his knee one morning. 'He said to the little Sap: "Put your foot on this," and then drew the outline of her foot with a pencil, saying "Tomorrow you'll have your shoes, but now pose a little more for me!" Sap, having tired of atomizer bottles and cardboard cats, had asked her "papa" for a pair of pumps. Every evening—ardent, happy but exhausted—Rodin would return to his hotel with his hands full of sketches and collect his thoughts.'

Photographs from the time show Rodin seated on a garden bench, sketching under the watchful eyes of the policemen who had been posted at the dancers' villa to ensure their safety. Rodin was oblivious: 'The friezes of Angkor were coming to life before my very eyes. I loved these Cambodian girls so much that I didn't know how to express my gratitude for the royal honour they had shown me in dancing and posing for me. I went to the Nouvelles Galeries to buy a basket of toys for them, and these divine children who dance for the gods hardly knew how to repay me for the happiness I had given them. They even talked about taking me with them.'

On their last day in France, hours before they boarded the ship that was to take them back to Cambodia, the dancers were taken to the celebrated photographer Baudouin. On the way, passing through a muddy alley, Princess Soumphady happened to step on a pat of cow-dung. Horrified she raised her arms to the heavens and flung herself, wailing, upon the dust, oblivious of her splendid costume. The rest of the troupe immediately followed suit; within moments the alley was full of prostrate Cambodian dancers, dressed in full performance regalia.

'What an emptiness they left for me!' wrote Rodin. 'When they left I thought they had taken away the beauty of the world. I followed them to Marseille; I would have followed them as far as Cairo.'

His sentiments were exactly mirrored by King Sisowath. 'I am deeply saddened to be leaving France,' the King said on the eve of his departure, 'in this beautiful country I shall leave behind a piece of my heart.'

9

The trip to France evidently cast King Sisowath's mind into the same kind of turmoil, the same tumult that has provoked generations of displaced students—the Gandhis, the Kenyattas, the

Chou en Lais, among thousands of their less illustrious countrymen—to reflect upon the unfamiliar, wintry worlds beyond the doors of their rented lodgings.

On 12 September 1906, shortly after their return to Cambodia, the King and his ministers published their reflections in a short but poignant document. Cast in the guise of a Royal Proclamation, it was, in fact, a venture into a kind of travel-writing. It began: 'The visits that His Majesty made to the great cities of France, his rapid examination of the institutions of that country, the organization of the different services that are to be found there, astonished him and led him to think of France as a paradise.'

Emulation, they concluded, was 'the only means of turning resolutely to the path of progress.'

Over the brief space of a couple of thousand words the King and his ministers summed up their views on the lessons that France had to offer Cambodia. Most of these had to do with what later came to be called 'development': communications had to be improved, new land cleared for agriculture; peasants had to increase their production, raise more animals, exploit their forests and fisheries more systematically, familiarize themselves with modern machinery and so on. A generation later, Cambodian political luminaries, such as Khieu Samphan, writing their theses in Paris, were to arrive at oddly similar conclusions, although by an entirely different route.

But it was on the subject of the ideal relationship between the state and its people, that the King and his ministers were at their most prescient: it was here, they thought, that Europe's most important lessons lay. 'None should hesitate to sacrifice his life,' they wrote, 'when it is a matter of the divinity of the King or of the country. The obligation to serve the country should be accepted without a murmur by the inhabitants of the kingdom; it is glorious to defend one's country. Are Europeans not constrained by the same obligation, without distinction either of rank or of family?'

Alas for poor King Sisowath, he was soon to learn that travel writing was an expensive indulgence for those who fell on his side of the colonial divide. In 1910 the Colonial Ministry in Paris wrote asking the King to reimburse the French government for certain expenses incurred during his trip to France. As it happened, Cambodia's budget had paid for the entire trip, including the dancers' performance at the Bois du Boulogne. In addition, the King, who was ruinously generous by nature, had personally handed out tips and gifts worth several thousands of francs. In return he and his entourage had received a few presents from French officials. Amongst these were a set of uniforms given by the Minister of Colonies and some rose-bushes that had been presented to the King personally at the Elysée Palace by none other than the President of the Republic, Armand Fallières. The French government now wanted to reclaim the price of the uniforms and the rose-bushes from the Cambodians.

For once, the obsequious Minister Thiounn took the King's side. He wrote back indignantly, refusing to pay for gifts that had been accepted in good faith.

The royal voyage to France found its most celebrated memorial in Rodin's sketches. The sketches were received with acclaim when they went on exhibition in 1907. After seeing them, the German poet Rilke wrote to the master to say, 'For me, these sketches were amongst the most profound of revelations.'

The revelation Rilke had in mind was of 'the mystery of Cambodian dance.' But it was probably the sculptor rather than the poet who sensed the real revelation of the encounter: of the power of Cambodia's involvement in the culture and politics of modernism, in all its promise and horror.

10

As for King Sisowath, the most significant thing he ever did was to authorize the founding of a high school where Cambodians could be educated on the French pattern. Known initially as the Collège du Protectorat, the school was renamed the Lycée Sisowath some years after the King's death.

The Lycée Sisowath was to become the crucible for Cambodia's re-making. A large number of the students who were radicalized in Paris in the fifties were graduates of the Lycée. Pol Pot himself was never a student there, but he was closely linked with it and several of his nearest associates were Sisowath alumni including his first wife, Khieu Ponnary, and his brother-in-law and long-time deputy, Ieng Sary.

Among the most prominent members of that group was Khieu Samphan, one-time President of Pol Pot's Democratic Kampuchea and now the best known of the Khmer Rouge's spokesmen. Through the sixties and early seventies Khieu Samphan was one of the pre-eminent political figures in Cambodia. He was renowned throughout the country as an incorruptible idealist: stories about his refusal to take bribes, even when begged by his impoverished mother, have passed into popular mythology. He was also an important economic thinker and theorist; his doctoral thesis on Cambodia's economy, written at the Sorbonne in the fifties, is still highly regarded. He vanished in 1967 and lived in the jungle through the long years of the Khmer Rouge's grim struggle, first against Prince Sihanouk, then against the rightist regime of General Lon Nol, when American planes subjected the countryside to saturation bombing.

Khieu Samphan surfaced again after the 1975 revolution as President of Pol Pot's Democratic Kampuchea. When the regime was driven out of power by the Vietnamese invasion of 1979, he fled with the rest of the ruling group to a stronghold on the Thai border.

As the Khmer Rouge's chief public spokesman and emissary he played a prominent part in the UN-sponsored peace negotiations from 1988 onwards. Later, in the months before this year's elections, it was he who was the Khmer Rouge's mouthpiece as it reneged on the peace agreements, while launching ever more vituperative attacks on the UN. The Khmer Rouge's manoeuvres did not come as a surprise to anyone who had ever dealt with its leadership: the surprise lay rather in the extent to which Untac was willing to go on appeasing them. Effectively, the Khmer Rouge succeeded in taking advantage of the UN's presence to augment its own military position while sabotaging the peace process.

Opposite: Khmer Rouge leader Khieu Samphang wearing an army helmet, and a pair of underpants as a bandage, after being assaulted by a mob which forced its way into the Khmer Rouge compound on his arrival in Phnom Penh on 27 Nov 1991.

In 1991 and 1992, when Khieu Samphan was travelling
und the world, making headlines, there was perhaps only a
gle soul in Phnom Penh who followed his activities with an
terest that was not wholly political: his forty-nine-year-old
ounger brother, Khieu Seng Kim.

I met Khieu Seng Kim one morning, standing by the
entrance to the school of classical dance. A tall man, with a cast
in one eye and untidy grizzled hair, he was immediately friendly,
eager both to talk about his family and to speak French. Within
minutes of our meeting we were sitting in his small apartment, on
opposite sides of a desk, surrounded by neat piles of French
textbooks and dog-eared copies of *Paris-Match*.

The brick wall behind Khieu Seng Kim was papered over
with pictures of relatives and dead ancestors. The largest was a
glossy magazine picture of his brother Khieu Samphan, taken
soon after the signing of the peace accords in 1991. He is
standing beside the assembled leaders of all the major
Cambodian factions: Prince Sihanouk, Son Sann of the centrist
Khmer People's National Liberation Front and Hun Sen of the
'State of Cambodia'. In the picture everybody exudes a sense of
relief, bonhomie and optimism; everyone is smiling, but no one
more than Khieu Samphan.

Khieu Seng Kim was a child in 1950, when his brother,
recently graduated from the Lycée Sisowath, left for Paris on a
scholarship. By the time he returned with his doctorate from the
Sorbonne, eight years later, Khieu Seng Kim was fourteen, and
the memory of going to Pochentong airport to receive his older
brother stayed fresh in his mind. 'We were very poor then,' he
said, 'and we couldn't afford to greet him with garlands and a
crown of flowers, like well-off people do. We just embraced and
hugged and all of us had tears flowing down our cheeks.'

In those days, in Cambodia, a doctorate from France was a
guarantee of a high-level job in the government, a means of
ensuring entry into the country's privileged classes. Their mother
would accept nothing less for herself and her family. She had
struggled against poverty most of her life; her husband, a
magistrate, had died early, leaving her five children to bring up
on her own. But when, despite her entreaties, her son refused to

accept any of the lucrative offers that came his way, once again she had to start selling vegetables to keep the family going. Khieu Seng Kim remembers seeing his adored brother—the brilliant economist with his degree from the Sorbonne—sitting beside his mother, helping her with her roadside stall.

In the meanwhile, Khieu Samphan also taught in a school, founded an influential left-wing journal and gradually rose to political prominence. He even served in Sihanouk's cabinet for a while, and with his success the family's situation eased a little.

And then came the day in 1967 when he melted into the jungle.

Khieu Seng Kim remembers the day well: it was Monday, 24 April 1967. His mother served dinner at seven-thirty and the two of them sat at the dining table and waited for Khieu Samphan to arrive: he always came home at about that time. They stayed there till eleven, without eating, listening for every footstep and every sound; then his mother broke down and began to cry. She cried all night, 'like a child who has lost its mother.'

At first they thought that Khieu Samphan had been arrested. They had good reason to, for Prince Sihanouk had made a speech two days before, denouncing Khieu Samphan and two close friends of his, the brothers Hu Nim and Hou Yuon. But no arrest was announced, and nor was there any other news the next day.

Khieu Seng Kim became a man possessed: he could not believe that the brother he worshipped would abandon his family; at that time he was their only means of support. He travelled all over the country, visiting friends and relatives, asking if they had any news of his brother. Nobody could tell him anything: it was only much later that he learned that Khieu Samphan had been smuggled out of the city in a farmer's cart the evening he failed to show up for dinner.

Eight years later, in 1975, when the first Khmer Rouge cadres marched into Phnom Penh, Khieu Seng Kim went rushing out into the streets and threw himself upon them, crying: 'My brother is Khieu Samphan, my brother is your leader.' They looked at him as though he were insane. 'The Revolution doesn't recognize families,' they said, brushing him off. He was driven out of the city with his wife and children and made to march to a work site just like everybody else.

Like most other evacuees Khieu Seng Kim drifted back towards Phnom Penh in 1979, after the Pol Pot regime had been overthrown by the Vietnamese invasion. He began working in a factory, but within a few months it emerged that he knew French and had worked as a journalist before the Revolution. The new government contacted him and invited him to take up a job as a journalist. He refused; he didn't want to be compromised or associate himself with the government in any way. Instead, he worked with the Department of Archaeology for a while as a restorer, and then took a teaching job at the School of Fine Arts.

'For that they're still suspicious of me,' he said, with a wry smile. 'Even now. That's why I live in a place like this, while everyone in the country is getting rich.'

He smiled and lit a cigarette; he seemed obscurely pleased at the thought of being excluded and pushed on to the edges of the wilderness that had claimed his brother decades ago. It never seemed to have occurred to him to reflect that there was probably no other country on earth where the brother of a man who had headed a genocidal regime would actually be invited to accept a job by the government that followed.

I liked Khieu Seng Kim, I liked his quirky younger-brotherishness. For his sake I wished his mother were still alive—that indomitable old woman who had spread out her mat and started selling vegetables on the street when she realized that her eldest son would have no qualms about sacrificing his entire family on the altar of his idealism. She would have reminded Khieu Seng Kim of a few home truths.

11

Khieu Samphan talked very little about his student days upon his return from France. He did however tell one story that imprinted itself vividly on his younger brother's mind. It had to do with an old friend, Hou Yuon.

Hou Yuon was initiated into radical politics at about the

same time as Khieu Samphan and Pol Pot; they all attended the same study groups in Paris; they did Party work together in Phnom Penh in the sixties, and all through the desperate years of the early seventies they fought together, shoulder-to-shoulder, in conditions of the most extreme hardship, with thousands of tons of bombs crashing down around them. So closely were Khieu Samphan and Hou Yuon linked, that along with a third friend, Hu Nim, they became a collective legend, known as the 'Three Ghosts'.

Once, at a Cambodian gathering in Paris, Hou Yuon made a speech criticizing the corruption and venality of Prince Sihanouk's regime. He was overheard by an official and soon afterwards his government scholarship was suspended for a year. Khieu Samphan's scholarship was suspended too as he was known to be Hou Yuon's particular friend.

To support themselves the two men began to sell bread. They would study during the day, and at night they would walk around the city hawking long loaves of French bread. With the money they earned, they paid for their upkeep and bought books; the loaves they couldn't sell they ate. It was a hard way to earn money, Khieu Samphan told his brother, but at the same time it was oddly exhilarating. Walking down those lamplit streets late at night, talking to each other, he and Hou Yuon somehow managed to leave behind the night-time of the spirit that had befallen them in Paris. They would walk all night long, with the fragrant, crusty loaves over their shoulders, looking into the windows of cafés and restaurants, talking about their lives and about the future.

When the revolution began, Hou Yuon was one of the first to die. His moderate views were sharply at odds with the ultra-radical, collectivist ideology of the ruling group. In August 1975, a few months after the Khmer Rouge took power, he addressed a crowd and vehemently criticized the policy of evacuating the cities. He is said to have been assassinated as he left the meeting, on the orders of the party's leadership. Hu Nim served for a while as Minister of Information. Then on 10 April 1977 he and his wife were taken into 'Interrogation Centre S-21'—the torture chambers at Tuol Sleng in Phnom Penh. He was executed several months later, after having confessed to being everything from a CIA agent

to a Vietnamese spy.

Khieu Samphan was then head of state. He is believed to have played an important role in planning the mass purges of that period.

For Khieu Samphan and Pol Pot, the deaths of Hou Yuon, Hu Nim and the thousands of others who were executed in torture chambers and execution grounds were not a contradiction but rather a proof of their own idealism and ideological purity. Terror was essential to their exercise of power. It was an integral part not merely of their coercive machinery, but of the moral order on which they built their regime; a part whose best description still lies in the line that Büchner, most prescient of playwrights, gave to Robespierre (a particular hero of Pol Pot's)—'Virtue is terror, and terror virtue'—words that might well serve as an epitaph for 'the twentieth century.

12

Those who were there then say there was a moment of epiphany in Phnom Penh in 1980. It occurred at a quiet, relatively obscure event: a festival at which classical Cambodian music and dance were performed for the first time since the revolution.

Dancers and musicians from all over the country travelled to Phnom Penh for the festival. Proeung Chhieng, one of the best-known dancers and choreographers in the country, was one of those who made the journey: he came to Phnom Penh from Kompong Thom where he had helped assemble a small troupe of dancers after the fall of Democratic Kampuchea. He himself had trained at the palace since his childhood, specializing in the role of Hanuman, the monkey-god of the Ramayana epic, a part that is one of the glories of Khmer dance. This training proved instrumental in Proeung Chhieng's survival: his expertise in clowning and mime helped him persuade the interrogators at his labour camp that he was an illiterate lunatic.

Opposite: A bed in Tuol Sleng, 'Interrogation Centre S-21', with cuffs for feet and hands.

At the festival he met many fellow-students and teachers for the first time since the revolution: 'We cried and laughed while we looked around to see who were the others who had survived. We would shout with joy: "You are still alive!" and then we would cry thinking of someone who had died.'

The performers were dismayed when they began preparing for the performance: large quantities of musical instruments, costumes and masks had been destroyed over the last few years. They had to improvise new costumes to perform in; instead of rich silks and brocades they used thin calico, produced by a government textile factory. The theatre was in relatively good shape, but there was an electricity crisis at the time, and the lighting was dim and unreliable.

But people flocked to the theatre the day the festival began. Onesta Carpene, a Catholic relief worker from Italy, was one of the handful of foreigners then living in Phnom Penh. She was astonished at the response: the city was in a shambles; there was debris everywhere, spilling out of the houses, on to the pavements; the streets were jammed with pillaged cars; there was no money and very little food—'I could not believe that in a situation like that people would be thinking of music and dance.' But still they came pouring in, and the theatre was filled far beyond its capacity. It was very hot inside.

Eva Mysliwiec, who had arrived recently to set up a Quaker relief mission, was at that first performance. When the first musicians came onstage she heard sobs all around her. Then, when the dancers appeared in their shabby, hastily-made costumes, suddenly, everyone was crying: old people, young people, soldiers, children—'you could have sailed out of there in a boat.'

The people who were sitting next to her said: 'We thought everything was lost, that we would never hear our music again, never see our dance.' They could not stop crying; people wept through the entire performance.

It was a kind of rebirth: a moment when the grief of survival became indistinguishable from the joy of living.

Parts of this article are based on reports in 1906 editions of *Le Petit Provençal*, *Le Petit Marseillais* and *Le Figaro*, and on the letters and documents in the following files in the Archives d'Outre-Mer at Aix-en-Provence: GGI 2576, 5822, 6643 and 15606. GGI 5822 contains a French translation of the royal proclamation on the king's voyage to France. The quotations in sections one and eight are from *Rodin et l'Extrême Orient*, (Paris, 1979) and from Frederic V.Grunefeld, *Rodin; A Biography*, (New York, 1987).

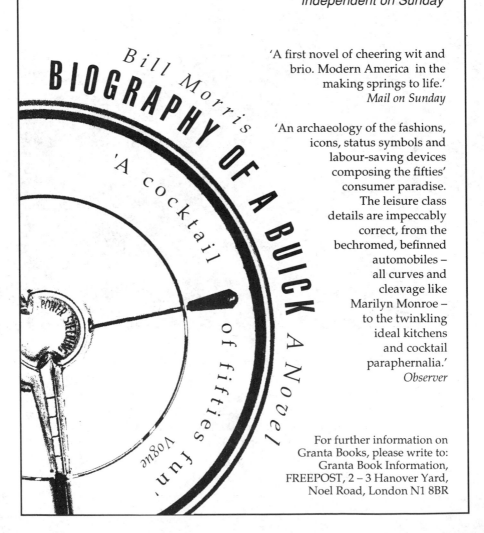

TOBIAS WOLFF
MEMORIAL

B.D. carried certain objects. He observed in his dispositions and arrangements a certain order, and became irritable and fearful when that order was disrupted. There were certain words he said to himself at certain moments, power words. Sometimes he really believed in all of this; other times he believed in nothing. But he was alive, and he gave honour to all possible causes.

His name was Benjamin Delano Sears, B.D. for short, but his friends in the unit had taken to calling him Biddy because of his fussiness and the hennish way he brooded over them. He always had to know where they were. He bugged them about taking their malaria pills and their salt tablets. When they were out in the bush he drove them crazy with equipment checks. He acted like a squad leader, which he wasn't and never would be, because Sergeant Holmes refused to consider him for the job. Sergeant Holmes had a number of sergeant-like sayings. One of them was, 'If you don't got what it takes, it'll take what you gots.' He had decided that B.D. didn't have what it took, and B.D. didn't argue; he knew even better than Sergeant Holmes how scared he was. He just wanted to get himself home, himself and his friends.

Most of them did get home. The unit had light casualties during B.D.'s tour, mainly through dumb luck. One by one B.D.'s friends rotated Stateside, and finally Ryan was the only one left. B.D. and Ryan had arrived the same week. They knew the same stories. The names of absent men and past operations and nowhere places had meaning for them, and those who came later began to regard the two of them as some kind of cultish remnant. And that was pretty much how B.D. and Ryan saw themselves.

They hadn't started off as friends. Ryan was a lip, a big mouth. He narrated whatever was happening, like a sportscaster, but the narration never fit what was going on. He'd complain when operations got cancelled, go into fey French-accented ecstasies over cold C-rats, offer elaborate professions of admiration for orders of the most transparent stupidity. At first B.D. thought he was a pain in the ass. Then one morning he woke up laughing at something Ryan had said the night before. They'd been setting out claymores.

Opposite: Tobias Wolff in 1965 at Fort Bragg. He served in Vietnam in 1967 and 1968.

173

Sergeant Holmes got exasperated fiddling with one of them and said, 'Any you boys gots a screwdriver?' and Ryan said, instantly, 'What size?' It was regulation blab but it worked on B.D. He kept hearing Ryan's voice, its crispness and competence, its almost perfect imitation of sanity.

What size?

Ryan and B.D. had about six weeks left to go when Lieutenant Puchinsky, their commanding officer, got transferred to battalion headquarters. Pinch Puchinsky saw himself as a star—he'd been a quarterback at Penn State, spoiled, coddled, illegally subsidized—and he took it for granted that other men would see him the same way. And they did. He never had to insist on an order and never thought to insist, because he couldn't imagine anyone refusing. He couldn't imagine anything disagreeable, in fact, and carried himself through every danger as if it had nothing to do with him. Because hardly any of his men got hurt, they held him in reverence.

So it was in the nature of things that his replacement, Lieutenant Dixon, should be despised, though he was not despicable. He was a proud, thoughtful man who had already been wounded twice and now found himself among soldiers whose laxity seemed perfectly calculated to finish him off. The men didn't maintain their weapons properly. They had no concept of radio discipline. On patrol they were careless and noisy and slow to react. Lieutenant Dixon took it upon himself to whip them into shape.

This proved hard going. He owned no patience or humour, no ease of command. He was short and balding; when he got worked up his face turned red and his voice broke into falsetto. Therefore the men called him Fudd. Ryan mimicked him relentlessly and with terrible precision. That Lieutenant Dixon should overhear him was inevitable, and it finally happened while Ryan and B.D. and some new guys were sandbagging the interior walls of a bunker. Ryan was holding forth in Lieutenant Dixon's voice when Lieutenant Dixon's head appeared in the doorway. Everyone saw him. But instead of shutting up, Ryan carried on as if he weren't there. B.D. kept his head down and his hands busy. At no time was he tempted to laugh.

'Ryan,' Lieutenant Dixon said, 'just what do you think you're doing?'

Still in the Lieutenant's voice, Ryan said, 'Packing sandbags, sir.'

Lieutenant Dixon watched him. He said, 'Ryan, is this your idea of a j-joke?'

'No, sir. My idea of a j-joke is a four-inch dick on a two-inch lieutenant.'

B.D. closed his eyes, and when he opened them Lieutenant Dixon was gone. He straightened up. 'Suave,' he said to Ryan.

Ryan shrugged. He pushed his shovel into the dirt and leaned against it. He untied the bandanna from his forehead and wiped the sweat from his face, from his thin shoulders and chest. His ribs showed. His skin was dead white, all but his hands and neck and face, which were densely freckled, almost black in the dimness of the bunker. 'I just can't help it,' he said.

Three nights later Lieutenant Dixon sent Ryan out on ambush with a bunch of new guys. This was strictly contrary to the arrangement observed by Lieutenant Puchinsky, whereby the shorter you got the less you had to do. You weren't supposed to get stuck with this kind of duty when you had less than two months to go. Lieutenant Dixon did not exactly order Ryan out. What he did instead was turn to him during the noon formation and ask if he'd like to volunteer. Ryan said that he would *love* to volunteer, that he'd been just *dying* to be asked. Lieutenant Dixon smiled and put his name down.

B.D. watched the detail go out that night. With blackened faces they moved silently through the perimeter, weaving a loopy path between mines and trip-flares, and crossed the desolate ground beyond the wire into the darkness of the trees. Above the trees the sky was a lilac haze.

B.D. went back to his bunk and sat there with his hands on his knees, staring at Ryan's bunk, at the mess on the sheets. Shaving gear, cigarettes, dirty clothes, sandals, a high school yearbook that Ryan liked to browse in. B.D. lifted the mosquito-netting and picked up the yearbook. *The Aloysian*, it was called. There was a formal portrait of Ryan in the senior class gallery. He looked solemn, almost mournful. His hair was long. The photographer had airbrushed the freckles out and used back-lights to brighten the outline of his head and shoulders. B.D. wouldn't have known him without the name. Below Ryan's picture was the line, 'O for a beakerful of the warm South!'

Now what the hell was that supposed to mean?

He found Ryan in a few group pictures. In one, taken in metal shop, Ryan was standing with some other boys behind the teacher, holding a tangle of antlerish rods above the teacher's head.

B.D. studied the picture. He was familiar with this expression, the plausible blandness worn like a mask over cunning and mockery. He put the book back on Ryan's bed.

His stomach hurt. It was a new pain, not sharp but steady, and so diffuse that B.D. had to probe with his fingers to find its source. When he bent over the pain got worse, then eased up when he stood and walked back and forth in front of his bunk. One of the new guys, a big Hawaiian, said, 'Hey Biddy, you OK?' B.D. stopped pacing. He had forgotten there was anyone else in the room. There was this Hawaiian and a guy with a green eye-shade and a bunch of others playing cards. They were all watching him.

B.D. said, 'Haven't you read the surgeon-general's warning?'

The Hawaiian looked down at his cigarette.

'Fuckin Biddy,' said the man with the eye-shade, as if B.D. weren't there. 'Eight months I've been in this shithole and he's still calling me *new guy*.'

'Ryan calls me Tonto,' the Hawaiian said. 'Do I look like an Indian? Seriously, man, do I look like an Indian?'

'You don't exactly look like a white man.'

'Yeah, well I don't *even* look like an Indian, OK?'

'Call him Kemo Sabe. See how he likes that.'

'Ryan? He'd love it.'

B.D. walked towards Sergeant Holmes's hooch. The sky was low and heavy. They'd had hamburgers that night for dinner; 'ratburgers,' Ryan called them—*Hey, Cookie, how about tucking in the tail on this one?*—and the air still smelled of grease. B.D. felt a sudden prickling coldness on his back and dropped to a crouch, waiting for something; he didn't know what. He heard men's voices, the chugging of generators, the crumple and thud of distant artillery, the uproarious din of insects. B.D. huddled there. And then he stood and looked around and went on his way.

Sergeant Holmes was stretched out on his bunk, listening to a big reel-to-reel through a set of earphones that covered his head like a helmet. He had on red Bermuda shorts. His eyes were closed, his long spidery fingers waving languorously over his sunken belly. He had the blackest skin B.D. had ever seen on anyone. B.D. sat down beside him and shook his foot. 'Hey,' he said. 'Hey, Russ.'

Sergeant Holmes opened his eyes. He took the earphones off.

'Dixon has no business sending Ryan out on ambush.'

Sergeant Holmes sat up and put the earphones on the floor. 'You wrong about that. That's what the man's business is, is sending people out.'

'Ryan's been out. Plenty. He's under two months now.'

'Same-same you, right?'

B.D. nodded.

'I see why you worried.'

'Fuck you,' B.D. said.

Sergeant Holmes grinned. It was an event in that black face.

'This goes against the deal, Russ.'

'Deal? What's this deal shit? You got something on paper?'

'It was understood.'

'Eltee Pinch gone, Biddy. Eltee Dixon head rat-catcher now, and he got his own different philosophy.'

'Philosophy,' B.D. said.

'That's how it is,' Sergeant Holmes said. 'That's the way.'

B.D. sat there, looking at the floor, rubbing his knuckles. He shook his head. 'What do you think?'

'I think Lieutenant Dixon in charge now.'

'The new guys can take care of themselves. *We* did.'

'You did shit, Biddy. You been duckin' ever since you got here, you and Ryan both.'

'We took our chances.'

'Hey, that's how it is, Biddy. You don't like it, talk to the eltee.' He put his earphones on, lay back on the bunk and closed his eyes. His fingers waved in the air like seaweed.

A few days later Lieutenant Dixon put together another ambush patrol. Before he read off the names he asked if one of the short-timers would like to volunteer. Nobody answered. Everyone was quiet, waiting, looking at him. Lieutenant Dixon studied his clipboard, wrote something and then looked up. 'Right. So who's going?' When no one spoke he said, 'Come on, it isn't all that bad. Is it, Ryan?'

B.D. was standing next to Ryan. 'Don't answer,' he told him.

'It's just great!' Ryan said. 'Nothing like it, sir. You've got your stars twinkling up there in God's heaven—'

'Thanks,' Lieutenant Dixon said.

'The trees for company—'

'Shut up,' B.D. said.

But Ryan kept at it until Lieutenant Dixon got impatient and cut him off. 'That's fine,' he said. He added, 'I'm glad to hear you like it so much.'

'Can't get enough of it, sir.'

Lieutenant Dixon slapped the clipboard against his leg. He did it again. He studied Ryan. 'Then I guess you wouldn't mind having another crack at it.'

'Gee, sir, can I?'

'I think it can be arranged.'

B.D. followed Ryan to their quarters after lunch. Ryan was laying out his gear. 'I know, I know,' he said to B.D. 'I just can't help it.'

'You can keep your mouth shut. You can stop hard-assing the little fuck.'

'The thing is, I can't. I try to but I can't.'

'Bullshit,' B.D. said, but he saw that Ryan meant it, and the knowledge made him tired. He lowered himself on to his bunk and lay back and stared up at the canvas roof. Sunlight spangled in a thousand little holes.

'He's such an asshole,' Ryan said. 'Somebody's got to brief him on that because he just doesn't get the picture, he doesn't have *any* hard intelligence on what an asshole he is. Somebody's got to take responsibility.'

'Nobody assigned you,' B.D. said.

'Individual initiative,' Ryan said. He sat down on his

footlocker and began to fiddle with the straps of his helmet.

B.D. closed his eyes. The air was hot and pressing and smelled of the canvas overhead, a smell that reminded him of summer camp.

'But that's not really it,' Ryan said. 'I'd just as soon let it drop. I think I've made my point.'

'Affirmative. Rest assured.'

'It's like I'm allergic, you know, like some people are with cats? I get near him, and boom, my heart starts pumping like crazy and all this stuff starts coming out. I'm just standing there, watching it happen. Strange, huh? Strange but true.'

'All you have to do,' B.D. said hopelessly, 'is keep quiet.'

The power of an M-26 fragmentation grenade, sufficient by itself to lift the roof off a small house, could be 'exponentially enhanced,' according to a leaflet issued by the base commander, 'by detonating it in the context of volatile substances.' This absurdly overwritten leaflet, intended as a warning against the enemy practice of slipping delay-rigged grenades into the gas tanks of unattended Jeeps and trucks, was incomprehensible to half the men in the division. But B.D. had understood it, and he'd kept it in mind.

His idea was to pick up a five-gallon can of diesel from one of the generators and leave it beside the tent where Lieutenant Dixon did his paperwork at night. He would tape down the handle of a grenade, pull the pin and drop the grenade in the can. By the time the gasoline ate through the tape he'd be in his bunk.

B.D. didn't think he had killed anyone yet. His company had been ambushed three times and B.D. had fired back with everyone else, but always hysterically and in a kind of fog. Something happened to his vision, it turned yellow and blurry and he saw everything in a series of stuttering frames that he could never afterwards remember clearly. He couldn't be sure what had happened. But he thought that he would know if he had killed someone, even if it was in darkness or behind cover where he couldn't see the man go down. He was sure that he would know.

Only once did he remember having somebody actually in his sights. This was during a sweep through an area that had been cleared of its population and declared a free-fire zone. Nobody was supposed to be there. All morning they worked their way upriver, searching the empty hamlets along the bank. Nothing. Negative booby traps, negative snipers, negative mines. Zilch. But then, while they were eating lunch, B.D. saw someone. He was on guard in the rear of the company when a man came out of the trees into an expanse of overgrown paddies. The man had a stick that he swung in front of him as he made his way with slow, halting steps towards the opposite tree line. B.D. kept still and watched him. The sun was warm on his back. The breeze blew across the paddies, bending the grass, rippling the water. Finally he raised his rifle and drew a bead on the man. He held him in his sights. He could have dropped him, easy as pie, but he had decided that the man was blind. He let him go and said nothing about it. But later he wondered. What if he wasn't blind? What if he was just a guy with a stick, taking his time? Either way, he had no business being there. B.D. felt funny about the whole thing. What if he was actually VC, what if he killed a bunch of Americans afterwards? He could be VC even if he *was* blind; he could be cadre, infrastructure, some sort of high official . . .

Blind people could do all kinds of things.

When it got dark, B.D. walked across the compound to one of the guard bunkers and palmed a grenade from an open crate while pretending to look for a man named Walcott.

He was about to leave when pumpkin-headed Captain Kroll appeared wheezing in the doorway. He had a normal enough body, maybe a little plump but nothing freakish, and then this incredible head. His head was so big that everyone in camp knew who he was and generally treated him with a tolerance he might not have enjoyed if his head had been a little smaller. 'Captain Head,' they called him, or just 'The Head'. He worked in battalion intelligence, which was good for a few laughs, and seemed not to know how big his head was.

Captain Kroll crouched on the floor and had everyone bunch up around him. B.D. saw no choice but to join in. Captain Kroll looked into each of their faces; it was like a football huddle. In a hushed voice he said that their reconnaissance patrols were reporting *beaucoup* troop movements all through the valley. They should maintain a *high* degree of alertness, he said. Mister Charles needed some scalps to show off in Paris. Mister Charles was looking for a party.

'Rock and roll!' said the guy behind B.D.

It was a dumbfuck thing to say. Nobody else said a word.

'Any questions?'

No questions.

Captain Kroll turned his big head from side to side. 'Get some,' he said.

Everyone broke out laughing.

Captain Kroll rocked back as if he'd been slapped, then stood and left the bunker. B.D. followed him outside and struck off in the opposite direction. The grenade knocked against his hip as he wandered, dull and thoughtless, across the compound. He didn't know where he was going until he got there.

Lieutenant Puchinsky was drinking beer with a couple of other officers. When B.D. asked to speak to him he called over his shoulder without looking: 'I already put my eight hours in. Tell Marston I'll give him the report tomorrow.'

B.D. stood in the doorway of the hooch. 'Sir, it's Biddy,' he said. 'Biddy Sears.'

'Biddy?' Lieutenant Puchinsky leaned forward and squinted at him. 'Christ. Biddy.' He put his can down.

They walked a little ways. Lieutenant Puchinsky gave off a certain ripeness, distinct but not rank, that B.D. had forgotten and now remembered and breathed in, taking comfort from it as he took comfort from the man's bulk, the great looming mass of him.

They stopped beside a cyclone fence enclosing a pit filled with crates. 'You must be getting pretty short,' Lieutenant Puchinsky said.

'Thirty-four and a wake-up.'

'I'm down to twenty.'

'Twenty. Jesus, sir. That's all right. I could handle twenty.'

A flare burst over the dead space outside the wire. Both men shrank from the sudden brightness. The flare drifted slowly down, hissing as it fell, covering the camp with a cold green light in which everything took on a helpless, cringing aspect. They didn't speak until it came to the ground.

'Ours,' Lieutenant Puchinsky said.

'Yes, sir,' B.D. said, though he knew this might not be true.

Lieutenant Puchinsky shifted from foot to foot.

'It's about Lieutenant Dixon, sir.'

'Oh, Christ, you're *not* going to tell me you're having trouble with Lieutenant Dixon.'

'Yes, sir.'

When Lieutenant Puchinsky asked him if he'd gone through channels, B.D. knew he'd already lost his case. He tried to explain the situation but couldn't find the right words and Lieutenant Puchinsky kept interrupting to say that it wasn't his outfit any more. He wouldn't even admit that an injustice had been done since, after all, Ryan had volunteered.

'Lieutenant Dixon made him,' B.D. said.

'How?'

'I can't explain, sir. He has a way.'

Lieutenant Puchinsky didn't say anything. He looked tired.

'We did what you wanted,' B.D. said. 'We kept our part of the deal.'

'There weren't any deals,' Lieutenant Puchinsky said. 'It sounds to me like you've got a personal problem, soldier. If your mission requires personal problems, we'll issue them to you. Is that clear?'

'Yes, sir.'

'If you're so worried about him, why don't *you* volunteer?'

B.D. came to attention, snapped a furiously correct salute and turned away.

'Hold up, Biddy.' Lieutenant Puchinsky walked over to him. 'What do you expect me to do? Put yourself in my place—what am I supposed to do?'

'You could talk to him.'

'It won't do any good, I guarantee you that.' When B.D. didn't answer, he said, 'All right. If it makes you feel any better I'll talk to him.'

B.D. did feel better, but not for long.

He had trouble sleeping that night, and as he lay in the darkness, eyes open, a rusty taste in his mouth, the extent of his failure became clear to him. He knew exactly what would happen. Lieutenant Puchinsky thought he was going to talk to Lieutenant

Dixon, and he would be loyal to this intention for maybe an hour or two, maybe even the rest of the night, and in the morning he'd forget it. He was an officer. Officers could look like men and talk like men, but when you drew the line they always went over to the officer side because that was what they were. Lieutenant Puchinsky had already decided that speaking to Lieutenant Dixon wouldn't make any difference. And he was right: it wouldn't. B.D. knew that. He understood that he had known it all along, that he had gone to Lieutenant Puchinsky in the first place so he wouldn't have to deal with Lieutenant Dixon afterwards. He had tipped his hand because he was afraid to play it, and now the chance was gone. In another week, ten days, the next time battalion sent down for an ambush party, Lieutenant Dixon was going to be out there asking for a volunteer, and Ryan was going to shoot off his mouth again.

And Lieutenant Puchinsky thought that he, B.D., should go out instead.

B.D. lay on his back a while, then turned on to his side. It was hot. Finally he got up and went to the doorway of the hooch. A new guy was sitting there in his boxer shorts, smoking a pipe. He nodded at B.D. but didn't say anything. There was no breeze. B.D. stood in the doorway, then went back inside and sat on his bunk.

B.D. wasn't brave. He knew that, as he knew other things about himself that he would not have believed a year ago. He would not have believed that he could walk past begging children and feel nothing. He would not have believed that he could become a frequenter of prostitutes. He would not have believed that he could become a whiner or a shirker. He had been forced to surrender certain pictures of himself that had once given him pride and a serene sense of entitlement to his existence, but the one picture he had not given up, and which had become essential, even sacred to him, was the picture of himself as a man who would do anything for a friend.

Anything meant anything. It could mean getting himself hurt or even killed. B.D. had some ideas as to how this might happen, acts of impulse like going after a wounded man, jumping on a grenade, other things he'd heard and read about, and in which he thought he recognized the possibilities of his own nature. But this was different.

In fact, B.D. could see a big difference. It was one thing to do something in the heat of the moment, another to have to think about it, accept it in advance. Anything meant anything, but B.D. never thought it would mean volunteering for an ambush party. He'd pulled that duty and he hated it worse than anything. You had to lie out there all night without moving. When you thought a couple of hours had gone by, it turned out to be fifteen minutes. You couldn't see a thing. You had to figure it all out with your ears, and every sound made you want to blow the whole place apart, but you couldn't because then they'd know where you were. Then they had you. Or else some friendly unit heard the firing and got spooked and called down artillery. That happened once when B.D. was out: some guys freaked and shot the shit out of some bushes, and it wasn't three minutes before the artillery started coming in. B.D. had been mortared but he'd never been under artillery before. Artillery was something else. Artillery was like the end of the world. It was a miracle he hadn't gotten killed—a miracle. He didn't know if he was up for that again. He didn't know if he could do this. He just didn't know.

B.D. rummaged in Ryan's stuff for some cigarettes. He lit one and puffed it without inhaling, blowing the smoke over his head; he hated the smell of it. The men around him slept on, their bodies pale and vague under the mosquito-netting. B.D. ground the cigarette out and lay down again.

He didn't know Ryan all that well, when you came right down to it. The things he knew about Ryan he could count on his fingers. Ryan was nineteen. He had four older sisters, no brothers, a girlfriend he never talked about. What he did like to talk about was driving up to New Hampshire with his buddies and fishing for trout. He was clumsy. He talked too much. He could eat anything, even gook food. He called the black guys Zulus but got along with them better than B.D., who claimed to be color-blind. His mother was dead. His father ran a hardware store and picked up the odd dollar singing nostalgic Irish songs at weddings and wakes. Ryan could do an imitation of his father singing that put B.D. right on the floor, every time. It was something he did with his eyebrows. Just thinking of it made B.D. laugh silently in the darkness.

Ryan was on a supply detail that weekend, completely routine, carrying ammunition forward from a dump in the rear, when a machine-gun opened fire from a low hill that was supposed to be secure. It caught Ryan and several other men as they were humping crates across a mud-field. The whole area went on alert. Perimeter guards were blasting away at the hill. Officers kept running by, shouting different orders. When B.D. heard about Ryan he left his position and took off running towards the LZ. There were two wounded men there, walking wounded, and a corpse in a bag, but Ryan was gone. He'd been lifted out with the other criticals a few minutes earlier. The medic on duty said that Ryan had taken a round just above the left eye, or maybe it was the right. He didn't know how serious it was, whether the bullet had hit him straight on or from the side.

B.D. looked up at the sky, at the dark, low, eddying clouds. He was conscious of the other men, and he clenched his jaw to show that he was keeping a tight lid on his feelings, as he was. Years later he told all this to the woman he lived with and would later marry, offering it to her as something important to know about him—how this great friend of his, Ryan, had gotten hit, and how he'd run to be with him and found him gone. He described the scene in the clearing, the wounded men sitting on tree stumps, muddy, dumb with shock, and the dead man in his bag, not stretched out like someone asleep but all balled up in the middle. A big lump. He described the churned-up ground, the jumble of boxes and canisters. The dark sky. And Ryan gone, just like that. His best friend.

This story did not come easily to B.D. He hardly ever talked about the war except in generalities, and then in a grudging, edgy way. He didn't want to sound like other men when they got on the subject, pulling a long face or laughing it off—striking a pose. He did not want to imply that he'd done more than he had done, or to say, as he believed, that he hadn't done enough; that all he had done was stay alive. When he thought about those days, the life he'd led since—working his way through school, starting a business, being a good friend to his friends, nursing his mother for three months while she died of cancer—all this dropped away as if it were nothing, and he felt as he had felt then, weak, corrupt and afraid.

So B.D. avoided the subject.

Still, he knew that his silence had become its own kind of pose, and that was why he told his girlfriend about Ryan. He wanted to be truthful with her. What a surprise, then, to have it all come out sounding like a lie. He couldn't get it right, couldn't put across what he had felt. He used the wrong words, words that somehow rang false, in sentimental cadences. The details sounded artful. His voice was halting and grave, self-aware, phony. It embarrassed him and he could see that it was embarrassing her, so he stopped. B.D. concluded that grief was impossible to describe.

But that was not why he failed. He failed because he had not felt grief that day, finding Ryan gone. He had felt delivered—set free. He couldn't recognize it, let alone admit it, but that's what it was, a strong, almost disabling sense of release. It took him by surprise but he fought it down, mastered it before he knew what it was, thinking it must be something else. He took charge of himself as necessity decreed. When the next chopper came in B.D. helped the medic put the corpse and the wounded men on board, and then he went back to his position. It was starting to rain.

A doctor in Qui Nhon did what he could for Ryan and then tagged him for shipment to Japan. That night they loaded him on to a C-141 med. evac. bound for Yakota, from there to be taken to the hospital at Zama. The ride was rough at first because of driving winds and the steep, almost corkscrew turns the pilot had to make to avoid groundfire from around the airfield. The nurses crouched in the aisle, gripping the frames of the berths as the plane pitched and yawed. The lights flickered. IV bags swung from their hooks. Men cried out. In this way they spiralled upwards until they gained the thin, cold, untroubled heights, and then the pilot set his course, and the men mostly quieted down, and the nurses went about their business.

One heard Ryan say something as she passed his cot. She knelt beside him and he said it again, a word she couldn't make out. She took his pulse, monitored his breathing: shallow but regular. The dressing across his forehead and face was soaked through. She changed it, but had to leave the seeping compress on the wound; the orders on the chart specified that no one should touch it until he reached a certain team of doctors in Zama. When she'd finished with the dressing the nurse began to wipe his face. 'Come on in,' Ryan said, and seized her hand.

It gave her a start. 'What?' she said.

He didn't speak again. She let him hold her hand until his grasp loosened, but when she tried to pull away he clamped down again. His lips moved soundlessly. In the berth next to Ryan's was a boy who'd had both feet blown off. He was asleep, or unconscious; she could see the rise and fall of his chest. His near hand was resting on the deck. She picked it up by the wrist, and when Ryan relaxed his grip again she gave him his neighbor's hand and withdrew her own. He didn't seem to know the difference. She wiped his face once more and went to help another nurse with a patient who kept trying to get up.

She wasn't sure exactly when Ryan died. He was alive at one moment, and when she stopped by again, not so long afterwards, he was gone. He still had the other boy's hand. She stood there and looked at them. She couldn't think what to do. Finally she went over to another nurse and took her aside. 'I'm going to need a little something after all,' she said.

The other nurse looked around and said, 'I don't have any.'

'Beth,' she said. 'Please.'

'Don't ask, OK? You made me promise.'

'Look . . . just this trip. It's all right—really, Beth, I mean it. It's all right.'

During a lull later on she stopped and leaned her forehead against a porthole. The sun was just above the horizon. The sky was clear, no clouds between her and the sea below, whose name she loved to hear the pilots say—the East China Sea. Through the crazed Plexiglas she could make out some small islands and the white glint of a ship in the apex of its wake. Someday she was going to take one of those cruises, by herself or maybe with some friends. Lie in the sun. Breathe the good air. Do nothing all day but eat and sleep and be clean, throw crumbs to the gulls and watch the dolphins play alongside the ship, diving and then leaping high to show off for the people at the rail, for her and her friends. She could see the whole thing. When she closed her eyes she could see the whole thing, perfectly.

GRANTA

IVAN KLÍMA
A CHILDHOOD IN TEREZIN

I am trying to reach, in memory, a time before the war began. What was I like then? I think that I inherited my mother's preference for solitude. We lived in a small villa on a road leading out of Prague, north of the most industrialized part of the city; my father worked as an engineer in one of the factories. There was another house down the road, and a pub catering to those who did not want to go thirsty into the centre, where they could expect to pay more for drinks. I had no brothers and sisters at the time; my brother was not born until I was seven. A girl about my age lived in our villa, and there was another boy slightly older than me living in the house down the road. I wasn't close to either of them, and though I did play with other children in the park, I had no close friends and spent most of my time alone with my toys. Children in those days were not surrounded by toys as they are now, so I can still remember most of mine. What sticks most firmly in my memory is a large curtain made from an old sheet, on which my mother had drawn Walt Disney's three little pigs. Behind this curtain we prepared plays with several stuffed animals for an audience that rarely showed up. From then on, puppet theatre became a passion, and before I grew up I made several of them, one in the concentration camp at Terezin.

Like many children, I was afraid of being alone in the dark, and before going to sleep I would ask for the door to the lighted hallway to be left open. Once in a while, when my parents went out for an evening, I would make a terrible fuss, although they never left me alone in the house; there was usually a maid.

When my mother first took me to school (I was two weeks short of turning six), it was one of the most terrifying experiences of my life. That day they let the parents stay in the classroom, by the door, and I spent the entire first lesson keeping an eye on my mother to make sure she had not abandoned me to the mercies of

Opposite: 'View of Terezin' by Petr Weidmann, who was born in 1930 and deported to Terezin on 20 November 1942. This drawing is dated '2 V 1944' and is one of a collection of children's drawings which were recovered from Terezin after the war. Petr Weidmann was deported to Auschwitz on 4 October 1944 where he was killed.

so many strange children and to the completely unknown woman forcing herself on my attention. Like most children, I did not enjoy school (in this sense, the war made my childhood dreams come true, for I was not allowed to go). But I learned well; I was quiet and longed for praise though I hardly ever volunteered to answer questions. When I was seven and had just got used to my classmates, we moved, and I had to get to know a whole new set. The Nazi laws did not permit me to start fourth grade.

Whether it was because I had no friends, or because what followed ruptured my life so completely, I don't know, but in any case I cannot recall a single face or the name of any classmates from that time.

M y mother and father both came from Jewish families, but my mother's family had adopted the Jewish faith by choice. In the seventeenth century only two religions were permitted in Bohemia: the Jewish and the Roman Catholic. Many Protestant congregations advised their members to adopt Judaism rather than Catholicism, probably reckoning, wrongly, that the ban was temporary and that under the cloak of Judaism they could keep their original faith alive. The temporary state of affairs persisted for more than a century and a half, and over that time, many former Protestants became Jews. I remember that even though my grandfather was a Marxist and a freethinker, he prayed every Friday evening in a language I couldn't understand. If my grandparents were freethinkers, my parents rejected not only religion, but their Jewish identity as well. My father believed that technology knew no borders and that therefore he was at home anywhere in the world. My mother thought of herself as a Czech and was proud of her Evangelical ancestors (she even had me baptized, and after the war I took an active part in the Evangelical youth movement). I mention this because until the beginning of the war I never heard the word 'Jew', not even as an insult. I did not know the Jewish holidays, and the rituals that punctuated my life were no different from those observed by other children.

At the age of seven, people aren't usually interested in politics, but I can still remember hearing Hitler's name crop up in household conversations and sensing a kind of shapeless monster lurking beneath it. My father used to listen to his speeches on the radio (my parents were fluent in German; I wasn't), and even to me the ranting voice sounded terrifying, though I understood not a single word. Then I learned that, for reasons I could not grasp, we would be moving to England, where my father had the promise of a job. I was worried about moving, but at the same time I looked forward to the long journey. I also received my first illustrated English textbook and mother began to learn English with me. My father wanted his mother to come with us, but her visa was held up, and then Hitler arrived, and soon after that the borders closed for the first time in my life—snapped shut like the doors of a cage or, more precisely, a trap.

In the summer of 1939 we moved for the last time, into Prague itself. Because the building we were to move into was still being completed, my father's aunt offered us accommodation. Aunt Teresa, the only rich person I knew, owned one of the most beautiful villas in Prague. (After the 1948 revolution the communists confiscated it; first the prime minister lived there, later the president himself.) Behind the villa was a magnificent garden built into the steep hillside of Troja. Aunt Teresa's daughter and her family also lived in the villa, and thus I came into contact with two of my distant cousins. The younger one, Kitty, was my age, and I formed my first childhood friendship with her. It seems odd now, for the Gestapo were already running the country and almost every week a new anti-Jewish statute was issued, but we children had no idea this was happening. We spent long, happy hours in the gazebo playing cards or mah-jong, gathering fruit or chasing each other around the garden. I could not have known that this would be my last holiday here for many years, and that three years later Kitty would step into a gas chamber.

My parents managed to hide the true state of affairs from me for another few months, though it is more likely they were hiding it from themselves, or rather, they could not really conceive of what was swiftly to follow.

There was one ban after another. First, I could not leave the city, then I could not go to school, to the theatre, to the movies, to the park or travel in the forward car of the tram.

About that time, Disney's *Snow White and the Seven Dwarfs* came to Prague. The temptation was too powerful to resist; I went and sat through the whole film in terror of being discovered and cruelly punished. How? I did not yet know. My experience did not yet include prison, and my imagination failed me. But the fear was all the greater because it had touched the unknown.

In the apartment building we eventually moved to were three Jewish families. Lucy, who lived on the ground floor, was slightly older than me, and Tommy, who lived two storeys above, was about a year younger. We befriended each other and played together. At that time, the habits of people living in the outskirts of Prague were like those of people in small towns and villages. On summer evenings, people would bring chairs outside on to the pavement and sit talking. Though all forms of entertainment were forbidden to us, we were not yet banned from this type of amusement—and we children would hang around close to those from whose midst we would soon be excluded, but who then had no objection to our presence. If some of them pitied us they were careful not to show it. Then one September day in 1941, Lucy came running up and told us, in tears, that her family was leaving on a transport to Poland. What was a transport? And where was Poland?

Lucy wept and said her farewells to everyone. One of the tenants even gave her a hug. The next day I saw the whole family lugging their suitcases down the street. No one ever saw them alive again. Tommy ended up in the gas chamber a little later.

The war began when I was two weeks short of my eighth birthday. I soon understood that the outcome of this war was something that immediately concerned my life, and even my survival. When the air-raid sirens went off, I would sit in the basement of our apartment block while the ack-ack pounded. I didn't know what the explosions meant; I hoped they were English bombs falling, while at the same time I was afraid that the bombs would fall on me and therefore I hoped they weren't bombs at all. I began to take an interest in the progress of the war. An enormous map of Europe and the northern shores of Africa hung on the wall of my room. I was not allowed to stick little flags or pins into the map, but every day I followed the shifting of the fronts. Dozens of local names have stuck in my memory and will remain with me till I die, names like Narvik and Trondheim, Dunkirk, Crete, Tobruk, Banghazi and El Alamein, Orel', Rostov or Voronezh. Many years after the war, when I began to collect old maps, I had an unconscious urge to look up all those old battle sites again—in Greece, in France, in the Ukraine or in the Libyan desert.

I was not allowed to go to school, and gradually most of the non-Jewish children began to avoid me. The beautiful Marcela, who lived in the neighbouring tenement house and whose father had declared himself a German (he wore a disgustingly flashy swastika in his lapel), began shouting 'Jew!' at me in the street. I didn't know exactly what she meant by it, but I felt ashamed all the same. When the edict came down that I was to wear a six-pointed star on my chest with JUDE written on it, I was even more embarrassed and preferred not to go out at all.

What was I to do at home all day? I read. Of all the books I owned, I was most excited by a prose translation of Homer's two epics. I read them over and over again, until I knew whole pages by heart. It did not occur to me until years later that, despite the story-teller's bias towards the Greeks, I sided passionately with the Trojans. I admired Hector and loved Paris for avenging his death: I too lived in a state of siege, and therefore I supported those who were themselves surrounded.

At the end of November 1941, my father was summoned to be transported. He didn't go to Poland, but had to take part in the preparation of a new camp in the fortified town of Terezin. Several days after that—it was 9 December 1941, exactly a half hour before noon (I remember that Mother was just cooking lunch)—Mother and I received our own summons. There was no mention of my brother, who was three. While others were given three days to prepare, they gave us only two hours.

Mother wept in terror and despair. What would become of my baby brother? While she was crying that she would rather kill herself, I tried to gather my things together and, with the help of neighbours, pack them into a suitcase. Among the essentials were three books: the volume of Homer, Dickens's *Pickwick Papers* and Verne's *The Children of Captain Grant.*

These books were to be my spiritual nourishment for the next three and a half years.

That afternoon, I became a real prisoner. I lost my name and was given a number, which of course I remember to this day: L54.

To most people, the incarceration (not to mention the murder) of children is one of the basest and most reprehensible of acts. While this is true, it doesn't say very much about the feelings of children in such a situation. Looking back on my experiences, I would say that I suffered less than the adults around me. Children are more adaptable than adults and they lack the ability (to a considerable extent, at least) to see things in perspective, to comprehend fully their conditions and circumstances. They also perceive space differently—what may seem an unbearable prison to an adult may be a large world to a child—because they have the capacity (as do women, to a far greater extent than men) to rank the inconsequential over the consequential, in other words, to delight in small things, or at least become absorbed by them, even at a time when they are threatened by death.

I recall the delight I felt when, after months of denial, I was once more sitting in a train, watching the countryside go by. I was actually looking forward to the change. I sensed that it would probably be for the worse, but I didn't think about it. I rejoiced that at the last minute they had brought my little brother to us, and that we would not have to be separated.

They placed us in rooms that belonged to the barracks of Terezin. Where ten or twelve soldiers had lived, about thirty-five women were to sleep. There was not a stick of furniture in the room. We put the cushions we had brought with us on the floor. Because there was not enough space, they had to be placed together lengthwise, two to a person. Simple tables were made from suitcases. The women, who mostly came from well-off families and were used to comfort (they had certainly never slept on a floor), were devastated by the new conditions. I can imagine how terribly some of them must have suffered: they were afraid for their children; they were plagued by insomnia, disease, discomfort and fear of the future. None of this bothered me at first. On the contrary, my new surroundings were full of adventure. My mood contrasted so sharply with their dejection that it enabled me to overcome my shyness and gain self-confidence. I helped the women carry in their baggage and move from place to place. I felt strong, capable of offering comfort. They listened to me; some even praised me; and however paradoxical it may sound, my newly won sense of importance in those unfamiliar surroundings made me feel almost happy.

Most of the women adapted incredibly quickly to the new, depressing living conditions. Soon songs and even laughter rang through the rooms. Above all they told stories, which I listened to with great delight.

Exactly a month after our arrival, the first transport left. No one knew where it was going, but we had come to treat each step into the unknown as a step towards something worse. The chosen women packed their suitcases again, wept and embraced those who, for the time being, remained behind. I was among those who stayed in the camp.

So much has already been recorded about prison life in the concentration camps of Germany and the former Soviet Union that I can only repeat what others have said. For three and a half years, I never saw so much as a morsel of fruit; I never ate a single egg, nor a gram of butter (at the time no one suspected the benefits of such a limited intake of cholesterol), not to mention chocolate or rice, a bun or a piece of carrot. Yet I don't recall that lack of food was what tormented or preoccupied me most. Nevertheless, food played a great role in the life of the internees and certainly, beyond the range of what I could see, they bartered and bribed with it in all sorts of ways.

My first love was also connected with food. The story I wrote about her (in the collection called *My First Loves*) is essentially autobiographical. I didn't even change her name, which was Myriam. Roughly a year before the end of the war, they began allotting the children a tiny amount (if I'm not mistaken it was a sixteenth of a litre daily) of skimmed milk. I was thirteen at the time, and the milk was distributed by a girl who might have been two or three years older than me. One day, instead of an eighth of a litre (for my brother and me), she gave me a portion at least four times that size. This went on day after day and I could imagine only one reason for this inexplicable generosity: the girl had fallen in love with me. This circumstance filled me with a happiness as powerful as it was unexpected. The horrors of concentration camp life all but vanished. I was bewildered and distracted. Myriam seemed to me more beautiful than all the other girls, but I never spoke to her. I merely hung around places where I could at least catch a glimpse of her. At the end of that summer, the Nazis nearly emptied the Terezin camp and sent most of the inmates to Auschwitz. Neither I nor my secret love were among those sent away, but my aunt, who had looked after food supplies in our barracks, was. As soon as she was gone, the extraordinary portions of milk dried up, which abruptly brought me down to the earth. Even so, I failed to see the connection between my aunt's departure and the cooling of the young milkmaid's ardour. It was only years later that I learned from my aunt, who survived Auschwitz, that she had ordered the girl to give me more milk. In my story, I tried to hint at this, but I obviously did it so subtly that not a single critic, nor any reader with whom I talked about the story, saw the connection. Perhaps that's as it should be: the mystery of the extra-large portions of milk remains as unresolved for them as it did all those years for me.

I was far more aware of the confinement than I was of the shortage of food. From the camp windows I could see the distant mountains and their inaccessibility. The fact that I could not go outside the gates of this crowded camp depressed me more than anything else. I remember once in the camp school (the school lasted only a few weeks, and then it was scattered to the winds by the transports) that we were given an assignment to write a composition on any subject of our choice. I wrote about the forest in Krc near Prague, and about the park on Petrin Hill; I wrote about trees, not people, because I didn't know much about people. Everyone I knew either shared my fate or was otherwise drowning in a world engulfed by war. Trees represented freedom.

Opposite: detail from 'Serving Meals' by Liana Franklová, who was born in Brno in 1931 and deported to Terezin on 5 December 1941. She was killed in Auschwitz on 19 October 1944.

The forest was associated with a tranquillity that had survived only in dreams.

My teacher showed her appreciation of the essay by asking me to read it out loud. Perhaps in doing so she helped determine my future calling. But it was more likely that as I was writing the composition, the liberating power that writing can give one was unexpectedly revealed to me. Writing enables you to enter places inaccessible in real life, even the most forbidden spaces. More than that, it allows you to invite guests along.

When you approach fourteen, you occasionally give some thought to what you want to do in life, and if you don't think about it yourself, others will do it for you, for life compels you to decide on a type of education or employment. In the camp, none of this applied. Like every prisoner, I was powerless to decide anything for myself and I accepted the fact. I was resigned to getting small amounts of miserable food, a piece of inferior soap and a bucket of coal in the winter; such things represented all that one could expect. The future posed only two questions: would I remain here, or would they take me away to places where people are never heard from again? And: when would the war end and would I manage to survive till then? The world in which a person gets an education, works, makes money and buys things with it was so remote as to be unreal.

Life in Terezin was not as strictly ordered as in other concentration camps. No one checked to see whether the barracks were properly cleaned, nor when those who were not required to work got up in the morning, or what they did during the day. Although everyone was constantly treading a thin line between being and non-being, the routine was, at the same time, wearingly monotonous. The day was punctuated by queues: for breakfast, lunch and supper; for the daily ration of bread, coal or margarine; for water, for the washroom or the toilet. The rest of the time we children had to ourselves. Oddly enough, we had a ball, and we would play ordinary games with it, most often volleyball or soccer. Perhaps because I had displayed a certain gift for ball games, I gained some status among my peers. I was appointed captain in most games, and in this new role my former shyness vanished. I also experienced my first real friendships at this time, which, as I later came to understand, were really only prefigurations of the adolescent infatuations that transform every encounter, every casual conversation into an experience of singular importance. All those friendships ended tragically; my friends, boys and girls, went to the gas chamber, all except one, the one I truly loved, Arieh, son of the chairman of the camp prisoners' self-management committee, who was shot at the age of twelve.

After the war, when I learned about the gas chambers, I often tried to imagine my friends at the moment when they knew there was no longer a way out and that they had to die. The thought has often awakened me in the middle of the night and terrified me far more than my memories of the evils I lived through myself.

Much has been written about the solidarity of prisoners, about how they surrendered their ration of food to someone who badly needed it. Such solidarity certainly existed, and I cannot remember, for instance, that anyone ever stole anything from anyone in our common living space. Yet stealing did go on in the camp at large, stealing of the most important thing of all: food. Even the extra portion of milk I was given over those few weeks was made possible only because someone else got a few drops less. My aunt, who worked in the noodle production plant, occasionally smuggled out a piece of rolled dough next to her body, and that too meant other prisoners had less. The women who worked in the gardening section sometimes spirited out a vegetable, but here they were stealing from our jailers. The punishment for all such thefts was transport, and thus death, yet it went on. I myself managed at times to steal a raw potato or a little coal, and once, a friend and I were able to break into the storage room containing luggage the SS guards had stolen from the prisoners, and I got away with a whole suitcase. This successful burglary was such an intense experience that to this day I recall almost everything I found in the suitcase: even the pattern on a pair of pyjamas.

This kind of thieving can certainly be explained by misery and hunger, but I think that my later experience with the communist regime persuaded me that the causes went deeper than that. The moment a criminal regime disrupts the norms of law, the moment crime is sanctioned, when some people, who are above the law, attempt to deprive others of their dignity and of their basic rights, people's morality is deeply affected. The criminal regime knows this and tries to maintain, through terror, the decent and moral behavior without which no society, not even a society governed by such a regime, can function. But it has been shown that terror can achieve little where people have lost the incentive to behave morally in the first place.

I filched the suitcase our murderers had stolen from someone else, and I was proud of my act, little appreciating how undignified my pride was.

In later years I came to realize that few things are harder to restore than lost honour, an impaired morality, and perhaps that was why I tried so hard to safeguard these things during the communist regime.

Every society that is founded on dishonesty and tolerates crime as an aspect of normal behaviour, be it only among a handful of the elect, while depriving another group, no matter how small, of its honour and even its right to life, condemns itself to moral degeneration and, ultimately, to collapse.

The memories of the success of the essays I read out in class remained with me. I wrote several short poems and started to write a novel which, if memory does not mislead me, had nothing to do with my life in the camp, but was about the American west. One of the prisoners who had taught Czech in schools before the war (I have no idea how she found out about my writing) offered to teach me in her free time. She laid out for me the principles of prosody, but theory remained theory, because books of poetry, as of prose, were virtually impossible to come by in Terezin.

Besides writing, I tried my hand at drawing. I was just as untrained in visual art as I was in literature, of course, and I had to work out the techniques of rendering perspective myself, but the fact that I was able to capture the likeness of the room where I lived filled me with satisfaction.

For a long time, I deplored having lost so much time in my education, but when I return to that time, after all these years, I would say that compared with the profusion of impressions, information and cultural (and pseudo-cultural) experiences that overwhelm young people today, I truly made the most of what little I encountered. I remember our puppet theatre, and a concert version of Smetana's *The Bartered Bride*. The presentation of this opera, which I should properly have seen as a child in the National Theatre in Prague, took place in our prison barracks. There was no orchestra, just the conductor, Mr Schaechter, accompanying the singers on a decrepit old harmonium. The singers, in their best clothes, performed standing on a low podium. I was crammed in with the rest of the audience, which listened in absolute rapture. I saw the tears in many eyes, and felt like crying myself. The experience was utterly intoxicating. Years later, when I went to see a proper production of the opera at the National Theatre, with costumes and an orchestra and chorus, I was disappointed not only by the music, but by the banality of the experience.

Hunger, and an enforced sojourn in an enclosed and closely guarded space, certainly made my childhood different from the childhood of most of my contemporaries, but what distinguished it most of all was the constant presence of death. People died in the room where I lived. They died by the dozen. Corpse carriers marched through my childhood, funeral wagons piled high with wooden boxes of unplaned, unpainted wood, wagons pushed and pulled by people, many of whom soon ended up on those wagons themselves. Every day, by the gates, I read long lists of those who had not lived to see the morning. The constant threat of the transports hung over us and, even though I knew nothing of the gas chambers, they seemed to carry people into a bottomless chasm. No one who ended up on a transport was ever heard from again. In the final days of the war, when they cleared out the camps in Poland and eastern Germany and brought the inmates to Terezin, I saw each day wagons piled with wretched corpses. From the sunken, sallow faces, stone-still eyes stared out at me, eyes that had had no one to close them. Stiffened arms and legs and bare scalps jutted against the sky.

When you live with death, you must, consciously or unconsciously, develop a kind of resolution. The knowledge that you can be murdered tomorrow evokes a longing to live intensively; the knowledge that the person you are talking to can be murdered tomorrow, someone you may be fond of, leads to a fear of intimacy. You build in yourself a kind of wall behind which you conceal what is fragile of yourself: your deepest feelings, your relationship to other people, especially to those closest to you. This is the only way to bear the repeated, despairing and inevitable partings.

If you construct such an inner wall when you are still a child, you must then spend the rest of your life tearing it down, and the question is, can you ever manage to destroy it completely?

With death walked fear. I knew that I was at the mercy of a force that had no feeling, a force that could do anything it wanted. I knew I could be included at any time in the transport and taken away to places from which there was no return. I knew that at any moment a man in a greyish-green uniform with a human skull on his cap could appear and beat or kill me.

An adult may accept fear and submit to it, or close himself to it. But a child has no real choice in the matter. A child can only cling desperately to a blind faith in the world in which it has grown up, that is, a fairytale world in which the forces of good triumph in a never ending battle with the forces of evil; where witches are outwitted and dragons beheaded. It seems paradoxical to talk of fairytales in the context of a concentration camp, but it was not just my peers and I who escaped into that world; the adults, whose powerlessness did not differ very much from ours, did so as well. Their world, like ours, was polarized into a primordial struggle between good and evil. It was a struggle in which our very lives were decided, and it took place somewhere in the distance, beyond our capacity to influence or affect it. Nevertheless—and I remember this very well—almost everyone believed good would prevail and that the war would soon be over. This faith helped them to sustain themselves and survive the humiliations, the anxiety, the disease and the hunger.

But the world, of course, is not a fairytale world, least of all at that time and in those places, and that sustaining faith proved hollow for most of the people around me. I, however, survived; I lived to see the end of it. For me, the forces of good, embodied chiefly in the Red Army, did in fact triumph, and it took me some time to understand fully that often it is not the forces of good and evil that do battle with each other, but merely two different evils, in competition for control of the world.

However, in prison-camp conditions a black-and-white vision of the world is reinforced by powerful emotional experiences. I longed for one moment so intensely that it seemed almost unreal: the moment of liberation.

Many people in our part of the world today suffer from the feeling that their lives lack excitement, a deeper happiness, and they try to find what they lack through drugs or mysticism. Few realize that a profound experience of happiness is impossible without an equally profound experience of deprivation.

To this day I remember every detail of the day when I stood by the razed prison fence, which I had once understood I would never be allowed to cross, and watched endless columns of Red Army soldiers, tired horses, exhausted people, dirty tanks, cars and cannons filed by, and for the first time I saw a portrait of Marshal Stalin, a man whose name I long afterwards associated with that moment, and I sobbed uncontrollably at the knowledge that I was free. As I watched, a German civilian was beaten to death, and a tank ran over a prisoner who too greedily flung himself on a pack of cigarettes someone had tossed on the ground, but none of this could spoil my mood or bring me down from the heights of my bliss. Years later, when I remembered my childhood and what had happened to me, an almost blasphemous thought occurred: that all those years of deprivation were worth that single, supreme sensation of freedom.

In a similar way, extraordinary moments of bliss purchased by long years of suffering often determine the lives not just of individuals but of whole nations. This is not necessarily something positive. On the contrary, the sensation of supreme happiness is the most transient of feelings, yet it can colour our judgement for a long time afterwards, despite the inevitable sobering up to follow, which causes deep frustration.

Sometimes when I think about my life and work, it occurs to me that for a writer, any experience, even the most drastic, is useful, should he survive it. By that I don't just mean that the most horrific experiences generally make for better story-telling than what routine life offers. Powerful and extreme experiences, when we stand on the very dividing line between life and death, or when, on the contrary, we know the bliss of sudden salvation, usually form us more clearly than anything else in life. But extreme experiences can unbalance our judgement. Seen from a point of disjunction, from a border line, the world usually appears to us as other than we normally perceive it. Questions of guilt and punishment, of freedom and oppression, of rights and lawlessness, of love and hate, of vengeance and forgiveness, seem quite simple, particularly in the eyes of a young person who has no other experience of life.

I recall how obsessed I was after the war with the idea of vengeance. Every day I listened breathlessly to live broadcasts of the many trials that took place at the time, of Czech collaborators as well as of the most prominent Nazis. I rejoiced in accounts of the executions of those condemned in the main trial in Nuremberg. I don't think I was very different from most of my contemporaries in this, but it wasn't long before I realized what the roots of those feelings really were, and that led me to reconsider my too simple judgements.

The realization I came to, and that I attempted to express in my prose, was this: the extraordinary experiences that we have gone through in this century as individuals and as groups can make us go badly astray. Moved by the desire to draw conclusions from our bitter experience, we are led to make fatal mistakes which, instead of bringing us closer to the state of freedom and justice we wish to achieve, take us in the opposite direction. In themselves, extreme circumstances do not open the way to wisdom. We can only achieve that if we are able to judge our experiences from a distance.

The events of childhood no doubt influence a person for the rest of his life. The relationship between them and what follows, however, is generally far from direct. I know people somewhat older than I was at the time who are permanently possessed by a feeling of paranoia, the expectation that what happened to them then can happen again at any time. In my case, the experience had an opposite effect. It seemed to me that what I had gone through could never be repeated, and the fact that I had survived filled me with an expectation, difficult to justify rationally, that I would happily survive everything I would ever encounter in life again. My wartime experience certainly helped me to survive, with a kind of distance, the years of persecution that dominated my adulthood.

If wartime experiences awakened in some people a longing for vengeance, it also hardened them for life towards anyone they considered an enemy, or even a potential opponent. Put simply, as victims of one kind of fanaticism, they often succumbed to fanaticism of an opposite kind.

With a certain distance, I have come to the conclusion that fanaticism of any kind is a psychological precondition, a precursor, of violence and terror; that there is no idea in the world good enough to justify a fanatical attempt to implement it. The only hope for the salvation of the world in our time is tolerance. On the other hand, those helpless, desperate multitudes driven, be it 'merely' into camps surrounded by wire and machine-gun towers, or directly into gas chambers or before firing squads, warn us that tolerance has its limitations. There is no disputing the fact that Hitler and his cronies (just as Lenin and his gang of revolutionaries) made no secret of their destructive intentions to limit the freedom of entire large groups of people, nor did they make any secret of their fanatical determination to achieve their ends regardless of the cost. If they had not encountered unpardonable indifference, hesitation and weakness, they might have been restrained. Tolerance must never mean tolerance of intolerance, tolerance of those who are prepared to limit the freedom or even the right to life, of anyone else, though it be justified by the most noble of ends.

I know that these are essentially simple principles, but over the years I have often been persuaded that it is precisely these truisms that are the hardest to uphold. Over and over again, we watch helplessly as multitudes march towards a fate prepared for them by some new mutation of fanaticism, one that we are, for mostly selfish reasons, prepared to tolerate, or at least publicly declare our helplessness to do anything about. Over and over again, we miss the moment when it might have been possible to end the violence without a great deal of bloodshed. Experience warns me that if we don't learn from catastrophes and if we don't accept these simple principles, the moment when we might have done something to decide the fate of mankind will pass us by.

Translated from the Czech by Paul Wilson

Picture copyright State Jewish Museum, Prague

Opposite: 'Checking for Lice' by Helga Weissová, who was born in 1929 and deported to Terezin with her parents in 1941. In October 1944 she was sent to Auschwitz and on from there to work camps; she and her mother survived the war. Helga Weissová-Hošková is now an artist and lives in Prague.

Art Film Theatre Sport Music Books Television Clubs

Time Out magazine

*The insider's guide to what's happening in London every day, every night.
Every week. £1.40*

GRANTA

PAUL THEROUX
CHATWIN REVISITED

When I think of Bruce Chatwin, who was my friend, I am always reminded of a particular night, a dinner at the Royal Geographical Society, hearing him speaking animatedly about various high mountains he had climbed. And that struck me as very odd, because I knew he had never been much of a mountaineer.

I was some way down the table but I heard him clearly. He spoke in his usual way, very rapidly and insistently, stuttering and interrupting and laughing, until he had commanded enough attention to begin speechifying. Being Chatwin, he did not stop at the peaks he scaled. He had plans for further assaults and expeditions—all of them one-man affairs, no oxygen, minimum equipment, rush the summit—and as he appeared to be holding his listeners spellbound (they were murmuring, 'Of course' and 'Extraordinary' and 'Quite right'), I peeked over to see their faces. On Chatwin's right was Chris Bonington, conqueror of Nanga Parbat and numerous other twenty-thousand footers, and on his left, Lord Hunt, leader of the first successful expedition up Everest.

'Chatter, chatter, chatter, Chatwin,' a mutual friend once said to me. He was smiling, but you could tell his head still hurt. Bruce had just been his house-guest for a week. 'He simply never stops.'

This talking was the most striking thing about him, yet there were so many other aspects of him that made an immediate impression. He was handsome, he had piercing eyes; he was very quick—full of nervous gestures, a rapid walker; he was often surprisingly mocking of the English. Of course, Bruce talks a lot, people said. It's because he's alone so much of the time. It was true that he was intensely solitary—he was given to sudden disappearances, that is, and everyone assumed he was alone. But even so, I believe he talked to himself, probably yakked non-stop, rehearsing his stories and practising funny accents and mimicry: it is a habit of many writers and travellers. I am sorry I never asked him whether he did this. I am sure he would have let out his screeching laugh and said, 'Constantly!'

He was such a darter he seldom stayed still long enough for anyone to sum him up, but when he died many people published

Photo: David Nash

Opposite: Bruce Chatwin in the Hindu Kush, 1964

their memories of him—and the portraits were so different. It was amazing how many people, old and young, many of them distinguished, a number of them glamorous, gathered to mourn him, in a Greek Orthodox church in London. Salman Rushdie sat in the pew in front of me with his then wife. It was Valentine's Day 1989, the day after the Ayatollah condemned Salman to death—I thought it was a hollow condemnation, and I joked about it. Judging from the congregation, Bruce had known everyone in London. But he had flitted from one to another, keeping people separate, making a point of not introducing them to each other, but often dropping their names.

He did not only drop Francis Bacon's name: he went one better and mimicked him—which suggested just how well he knew him. 'Oh, dear,' he would say, with an epicene hiss, 'a million quid for one of my paintings—I'll just spend it on champagne.' He could get two or three boasts into a single statement, as in, 'Werner Herzog and I just hiked two hundred miles in Dahomey,' or, 'David Hockney told me that his favourite painter is Liotard, a seventeenth-century Swiss. He's brilliant. I often go to the Rijksmuseum just to look at his work.' (This must have been true, because one day in Amsterdam, Bruce showed me a Liotard painting.)

Postcards are the preferred medium for many boasters, combining vividness, cheapness and an economy of effort—something like a miniature billboard. Bruce was a great sender of postcards. He sent them to me from France, from China, from Australia and from the artists' colony, Yaddo—*Feverish lesbian sculptors doing vulvaic iconography in plastic.* He encapsulated a theory about an Italian writer in Yunnan. From Australia he wrote, *You must come here. The men are awful, like bits of cardboard, but the women are splendid.* And on another postcard (this one of a bushranger), *Have become interested in an extreme situation—of Spanish monks in an Aboriginal mission and am about to start sketching an outline. Anyway the crisis of the 'shall-never-write-another-line' sort is now over.*

In terms of writing, he was in a state of permanent crisis. Perhaps he had started to write too late in his life, perhaps he lacked confidence. A writer talking to another writer about the difficulty of writing is hardly riveting. Bruce was at his least interesting bemoaning his writer's block, and I often felt that he was not really bemoaning it at all, but rather boasting about the subtlety of his special gift, the implication being that it was so finely tuned it occasionally emitted a high-pitched squeal and seemed to go dead; but no, it was still pulsing like a laser—it had simply drifted an instant from his sights. I had no such story to tell—I was producing a book a year, turning the big wooden crank on my chomping meatgrinder. How could I talk about a literary crisis, when all I had to do was grab the crank and give it a spin?

He did write like an angel most of the time, but he is never more Chatwinesque than when he is yielding to his conceit. In *The Songlines* he mentions being in Vienna speaking with Konrad Lorenz (in itself something of a boast) on the subject of aggression. Considering that Lorenz is the author of *On Aggression*, this was audacious of Bruce, but he was unfazed in the presence of the master, and went further, cheerfully adumbrating his own theories of aggression ('But surely,' he asked pointedly, 'haven't we got the concepts of "aggression" and "defence" mixed up?'), implying that Konrad Lorenz had been barking up the wrong tree in sixty-odd years of scientific research. Bruce then sketches his Beast Theory: mankind needing to see his enemy as a beast in order to overcome him; or needing to be a 'surrogate beast' in order to see men as prey.

It seems astonishing that the renowned zoologist and philosopher did not find Bruce's theory conventional and obvious (as it sounds to me). Instead, 'Lorenz tugged at his beard, gave me a searching look and said, ironically or not I'll never know: "What you have just said is totally new."'

Chatwin claimed to have the usual English disdain for flattery and praise, which is odd, because he adored it, and of course—praise is cheap and plentiful—it was lavished upon him. To need praise is human enough. Bruce solicited it by circulating to his friends bound proof copies of his books. We would read them and scribble remarks in the margin. I remember the scribbled-over copy of *The Viceroy of Ouidah*. My remarks were anodyne, but some other snippets of marginalia were shrieks of derision: 'Ha! Ha!' or 'Rubbish' or 'Impossible!' He said he didn't care.

Here he is in Dahomey, speaking to an African soldier, in his sketch, 'A Coup':

'You are English?'

'Yes.'

'But you speak excellent French.'

'Passable,' I said.

'With a Parisian accent I should have said.'

'I have lived in Paris.'

Much of his reading was in French, usually obscure books. It would be something like Rousseau's *Des rêveries du promeneur solitaire*, Gide's *Nourritures terrestres*, Rimbaud's *Les Illuminations* or—one of the strangest travel books ever written—*Voyage au tour de ma chambre*. When he found a book that few other people had read he tended to overpraise it. He might dismiss a book precisely because it was popular.

His ability to speak French well was of course part of his gift for mimicry, and it delighted me, though it irritated many who felt Bruce was showing off. When he appeared on the Parisian literary television show *Apostrophe*, he was interviewed in French and he replied with complete fluency, talking a mile a minute.

He was full of theories. One was highly complex and concerned the origin of the colour red as the official colour of Marxism. This theory took you across the ocean to Uruguay. It involved butchers in Montevideo, peasants on horseback, Garibaldi and the Colorado Party. I think I've got that right. The theory then whisked you back to Europe, to Italy, to Germany, to Russia and to the adoption of—was it an apron? was it a flag? It was all very confusing, though Chatwin told the story with precision, and always the same way. I know this because I heard him explain the theory at least four times. He told it to everyone. It was tiresome to hear this theory repeated, but it was even more annoying to realize that he had not remembered that he had told you before.

That was something his friends had to endure. If he couldn't recall that he was repeating something to you verbatim—shrieking each predictable thing and looking eager and hopeful—that seemed to indicate that he cared more about the monologuing itself than about you. The worst aspect of bores—even part-timers like Bruce—is their impartiality, their utter lack of interest in whoever they happen to be drilling into. Because it hardly matters who they are with, they victimize everyone, great and small.

Bruce was a fairly bad listener. If you told him something he would quickly say that he knew it already; and he would go on talking. Usually he was such a good talker that it hardly mattered.

But while most of us knew his stories, there were always great gaps in between them. There is an English saying which expresses befuddlement, *Who's he when he's at home?* Exactly. Everyone knew Bruce was married—we had met his wife, Elizabeth. But what sort of marriage was this? 'A *mariage blanc*,' a friend once said to me, pursing his lips. Bruce was in his way devoted to his wife, but the very fact of Bruce having a wife was so improbable that no one quite believed it.

One night at dinner, just before he left the table, I heard Bruce distinctly speak of his plans for the near future and say, 'I'm going to meet my wife in Tibet.' Afterwards, one of the people present said, 'Did he say his wife was dead?' and another replied, 'No. He said his wife's in bed.'

He kept so much to himself. We heard the colourful stories of a born raconteur. But what of the rest of it? We wondered what his private life was really like, and sometimes we speculated. His first book, *In Patagonia*, embodied all his faults and virtues. It was highly original, courageous and vividly written. He inscribed a copy to me, writing generously, *To Paul Theroux, who unwittingly triggered this off* (and he explained that a book of mine had inspired him). But his book was full of gaps. How had he travelled from here to there? How had he met this or that person? Life was never so neat as Bruce made out. What of the other, small, telling details, which to me give a book reality?

I used to look for links between the chapters, and between two conversations or pieces of geography. Why hadn't he put them in?

'Why do you think it matters?' he said to me.

'Because it's interesting,' I said. 'And because I think when you're writing a travel book you have to come clean.'

This made him laugh, and then he said something that I have always taken to be a pronouncement that was very near to being his motto. He said—he screeched—'I don't believe in coming clean!'

We had a mutual friend, an older and distinguished writer who felt that Bruce was trying to live down the shame of being the son of a Birmingham lawyer. I challenged this.

The man said, 'No. You're wrong. Look at Noel Coward. His mother kept a lodging house. And he pretended to be so grand—that theatrical English accent. All that posturing. He knew he was common. It was all a pretence. Think of his pain.'

This might have been true in a small way of Bruce, but I think that he was secretive by nature. It kept him aloof. It helped him in his flitting around. He never revealed himself totally to anyone, as far as I know, and in this way he kept his personality intact. In any case, he never struck me as being thoroughly English. He was more cosmopolitan—liking France, feeling liberated in America, being fascinated by Russia and China, something of a cultural exile.

I am skirting the subject of his sexual preference because it does not seem to me that it should matter. Yet it was obvious to anyone who knew him that in speaking tenderly of marital bliss he was always suppressing a secret and more lively belief in homosexuality. That he was homosexual bothered no one; that he never spoke about it was rather disturbing.

In an ungracious memoir, the writer David Plante refused to see Bruce's sense of fun and perhaps even deeper sense of insecurity. Plante wrote at length about how they had gone to a gay disco in London called 'Heaven', but it is characteristic of the memoir's dark hints and hypocrisy that Bruce's behaviour is regarded as sneaky and insincere, while Plante himself never discloses his own motive for going to the gay hangout.

I wanted to know more about his homosexual life, not because I am prurient but because if I like someone I want to know everything. And while Bruce was exasperated by others who kept their secrets, he was secretive himself. He never wrote about his sexuality, and some of us have laid our souls bare.

When he called me he always did so out of the blue. I liked that. I liked the suddenness of it—it suited my life and my writing. I hated making plans for the future. I might not be in the mood that far off day; I might be trying to write something. If he called in the morning, it was always a proposal to meet that afternoon or evening. And then I might not hear from him for six months or a year.

It surprised me that he had agreed to give a lecture for the Royal Geographical Society, but he had done it on one condition—that it be a duet. Would I agree? I said OK, and I quickly realized we were both doing it so as to seem respectable among all these distinguished explorers and travellers

Working together with him to prepare the lecture I realized how little I knew him and what an odd fish he was. He was insecure, I knew that, and it had the effect of making him seem domineering. 'I can't believe you haven't read Pigafetta,' he would say, and he would put the book in my hand and insist I read it by tomorrow; and the next day he would say, 'Our talk's going to be awful, it's hopeless, I don't know why we agreed to do this;' and later on would say, 'By the way, I've invited Sally, Duchess of Westminster.'

I found this maddening. I felt it was a task we had to perform, and that we would do it well if we were decently prepared. Bruce's moods ranged from rather tiresome high spirits to days of belittling gloom. 'No one's going to come,' he said. 'I'm certainly not inviting anyone.'

We got in touch with a dozen members of the RGS who had photographs of Patagonia, and we assembled eighty or a hundred beautiful pictures of the plains, of glaciers, of penguins, of snow and storms.

When the day came it turned out that Bruce had invited many people, including his parents—his big beefy-faced father had the look of a Dickensian solicitor—and he was miffed that the Duchess hadn't been able to make it. The lecture itself I thought was splendid—not so much for the text but for the atmosphere, the oddity. We gave it in the wooden amphitheatre, where so many distinguished explorers had reported back to the society; and we stood in the dark—a little light shining on our notes, while big beautiful pictures of Patagonia flashed on the screen behind us. This was thrilling—just our voices and these vivid Patagonian sights.

There was loud applause afterwards. Bruce, who would have been a wonderful actor, was flushed with pleasure. He had been brilliant, and I realized that he had needed me to encourage him and get him through it.

And when I heard him at dinner regaling Lord Hunt and Chris Bonington with his mountaineering exploits I thought: He's flying!

He travelled. We ran into each other in various places—in America, in Amsterdam. When he wanted to meet someone I knew well he simply asked me to introduce him. Graham Greene he particularly wanted to meet. But Bruce was disappointed. He thought Greene was gaga. He could not understand the mystique. He loved Borges. Later he needed glamour. He let himself be courted by Robert Mapplethorpe. He liked the thought of his portrait appearing in Mapplethorpe's notorious exhibition, along with photographs of women weight-lifters and strange flowers and even stranger sexual practices.

He went to China—just a magazine assignment, but Bruce made it seem as though he had been sent on an expedition by the Royal Geographical Society. I admired that in him. He took his writing assignments seriously, no matter who he was writing for. He was the opposite of a hack, which is to say something of a pedant, but a likeable one, who was fastidious and truly knowledgeable.

When he fell deathly ill soon after his China trip, the word spread that he had been bitten by a fruit bat in Yunnan and contracted a rare blood disease. Only two other people in the entire world had ever had it, so the story went, and both had died. Bruce was near death, but he fought back and survived. And he had another story to tell at dinner parties—of being bitten by a Chinese bat. He recovered. A friend said to me, 'I just saw Bruce walking through Eaton Square carrying a white truffle.'

But the blood disease returned. 'I was warned that it might pop up again,' Bruce explained. What kind of bat was this exactly? Bruce was vague, and he became very ill. Seeing him was like looking at the sunken cheeks and wasted flesh of a castaway. That image came to me again and again, the image of an abandoned traveller—the worst fate for travellers is that they become lost, and instead of revelling in oblivion, they fret and fall ill.

When I visited his bedroom in Oxfordshire—a pretty, homely farmhouse that Elizabeth kept ticking over—his hands would fly to his face, covering his hollow cheeks.

'God, you're healthy,' he would say sadly. But later he would cheer up, making plans. 'I'm going to California to see Lisa Lyon. She's fabulous. The woman weight-lifter? You'd love her.' And when I prepared to go, he would say, 'I'm not ready for *The Tibetan Book of the Dead* yet.'

'He expected to get better, and when he got worse he was demoralized and just let go,' Elizabeth told me. 'He was in terrible pain, but at the height of it he lapsed into a coma, and that was almost a blessing.'

Hovering in this fragile state of health he died suddenly. He had been handsome, calculating and demanding; he was famous for his disappearances. His death was like that, just as sudden, like Bruce on another journey. We were used to his vanishings—his silences could be as conspicuous as his talk. It seems strange, but not unlike him, that he has been gone so long.

Now, here's the good news.

Britain's New National Cartoon Newspaper
Out Now and Every Fortnight. £1.20.

GRANTA

BRUCE CHATWIN
THE ROAD TO OUIDAH

2 January 1971, Hotel du Sahel, Niamey, Niger. The usual horror of air travel. Packaged and processed on a death cart, let down at an African airport that one might mistake for the moon, swindled by the taxi-driver and porter and installed in one of those anonymous hotels with white tiles, angular leatherette-covered furniture, gleaming chromium. From the window, a terrace with limp, feathery acacias and the Niger valley rising beyond.

Wandered in the town, to the museum and zoo. These capitals of Africa are quite formless, isolated concrete villas in acacia plantations and jacaranda trees. The African smile—slow, stupid, full of good nature. The procession of women moving up and down with their baskets. The sense of balance is amazing. Tiny little woman with shrivelled breasts carrying a pair of calabashes full of millet flour. The degree to which an African mother is a self-contained unit—feeder, etc. Thin legs walking on dusty pavements. All the cars save for taxis are driven by Europeans. Europe wealth glittering. No excitement, merely a dull lethargy.

Sore feet. The basketball boots bought at great expense in London pinch the toes. I believe I have curiously deformed feet.

Don't admire this culture very much. Pure asceticism of the desert appeals to my arid sense far more.

Huge blackened cauldrons. The booths—one a reddish contraption of flattened tin cans and wood painted maroon. Scrawled across it in white painted lettering *lait frais et lait caidé Amadou Adina No 1.*

Bruce Chatwin, who died on 18 January 1989 at the age of forty-eight, left behind more than fifty pocket-sized moleskin notebooks and exercise books. The books are not so much diaries as a reference library of on-the-spot observation, the literary equivalent of a painter's sketchbook, written for later use and for the author's eyes only. The selection that follows describes the journey Chatwin made from Niger through the country of Dahomey and on to the city of Ouidah on the West African coast. Chatwin was also a photographer, and many of his pictures will be published in Britain for the first time in the *Telegraph Magazine* on 9 October 1993.

The barkers seem to be a caste of Hausas from Nigeria. Their booths are plastered with posters of the country's 'National Rulers'. Very preoccupied with unity. 'Unity is Strength.'

The French always export the very worst of their culture to the colonies. Yet the combination is not displeasing.

Meat-sellers with hurricane lamps. Umbilical hernias protrude from the bellies of children like some strange tropical fruit.

A restaurant in a garden. I drank a beer on a red spotted cloth-covered table. Mosquitoes bit the hard parts of my fingers. Cool, even quite cold. My backache has completely disappeared. For such small mercies one can be thankful. *Il n'y a personne.* Sometimes there are people, sometimes none at all, says the boy. Yet the menu has fresh caviar, blinis, *terrine de faisan* etc. A tart came up to the next table and began slapping a Frenchman in a yellow shirt patterned with Tahiti-style Pacific fronds.

The sunset left an afterglow. Bands in the sky dark indigo to grey to soft rose. Hills on the other side of the river two shades of grey. The light of the sky reflected in the river.

The smell of Africa.

The American party at the next table. He announced himself very grandly as the Deputy Director of the Peace Corps, so signifying I had no right to address more than a few words to such a person. Their conversation was banal to the point of fascination. It centred on the merits of this or that Jewish comedian on American TV. Both women are tough and pointless, the men are ineffectual. Very straight and square and they want to know Vice-President Agnew and help the blacks. Poor blacks.

Where can a man go to be free of this chit-chat?

I am going home to the hotel.

7 January. Bus journey to N'konni. Niger olive green. Peuls in hats hacking up the road. Piles of peanuts arranged in conical heaps. Rocks in the river. Green islands of vegetation floating downstream. Land the greenish ochre colour of a lion. Villages like mushrooms. Skeletal trees in the heat haze.

A pair of Moorish marabouts travelling. They come from Néma in Mauretania and seem pleased to have been there. They travel for six months of the year. Their next stay is in Néma. One

('*Un grand marabout*,' he confides) will go to the sheikhdoms of the Cameroons. His companion has the startling physiognomy I have noticed among the Moors. High cheeks, long well-formed jaw and sharp pointed chin emphasized by a goatee. Elegance of the Moors. Clean ascetic quality of Islam. The smell of course is less than anything one might expect on a European bus.

The driver, tough, wearing a leather jacket and a red and white checked turban over most of his face. Dark glasses give him total protection.

The women tugging at strips of sugar cane, peeling great strips off like the sound of sticking paper. Heat cannot suppress the female conversation. Child with huge gold earrings. What age do they pierce the ears?

Passed huge Ali-Baba-jar granaries raised on stilts like giant ostriches. Green powder-puffs of trees. Horses feeding on bleached grass. Red roads of Africa. The advertisement for Bière Nigérienne carries a photo of a blonde. Someone with a powerful sweet smell has come into the bus. Voyages bring out the best in people—this voyage brought out the worst in me.

Birnin N'konni. Arrived here in the dark and dined in a pea-green painted restaurant called Le Lotus Bleu. *La Patronne* was a Vietnamese-Negro half-caste who kept a few Vietnamese dishes on her menu as a tribute to her oriental past. Then taken by a charming self-deprecating Martiniquais who wore a bright scarlet shirt and had been a student in Nanterre in 1968 at the time of the *événements*. His friend spent the whole night buried in my book by the light of a spirit-lamp.

Chez Vietnam. Concrete balustrade and black women coming up the ochre landscape with half moon calabashes, light blue wraps covering the ends of their breasts hanging down like envelopes flattened. The Hausas have scarifications like cat-whiskers. Scarifications make the face into an artificial landscape, intersecting the natural contours. Peuls have little blue triangles low down the cheeks. Rich men in lavender-blue cotton *boubous*, caps in orange, bright colours, chequered bright. Kites and feathery foliage. Mud walls. The red dust whipped up in the wind gets in the eyes and hair. It makes the hair wire-stiff. The boy who looked as if he had red hair till I saw it was the dust all over it.

Gutted cars like carcasses of animals. Dogs look as though they're dead—bleached out. The *patronne*'s dust-coloured poodle. Straight bristly hair. Her tiny little feet and bow-legs that go in at the kneecaps like hourglasses.

Football the boys were playing. When one kicked the ball, the other would go flying round in a circle pirouette.

Bearded Frenchman and a friend entered. Delighted, the woman screamed with joy and said she had a sausage specially for him. He didn't want a sausage but he wanted *café au lait* and she promised him *un bon bifteck bordelais* but he still said he wanted a *café au lait*. Beard parted in the middle almost like the wings of a butterfly.

Face came over the wall—a Peul, sharp featured in a straw hat that looked like an old-fashioned beehive, and a mouth filled with teeth chewing pinkish cola nuts which came away in little pieces in the wind as he spoke.

Touareg boy with a regular brown handsome face and close cropped hair. He stayed still, silent, grave like a sculpture until he smiled—flashed friendly quick smile—then went silent again and grave. Walked round the edge of the room for fear of disturbing anything in the middle. His boss the Martiniquais played a flute during the night. He wasn't very good at it.

Tomorrow in search of Peuls to a market called Tamaské.

Tamaské. My travelling companion is a charming girl student at the École des Hautes Études at Zinder. She is naturally on strike against the greed of President Pompidou who will leave today on his round to shore up the mineral reserves of France. Niger is the world's third largest exporter of uranium. Ten per cent for Niger, eighty per cent for France.

Open-air markets under trees. Goatskin sacks, some adorned with green leather clips. Village idiots lying in the dust in heaps with their shirts pulled over their heads to protect them from the sun, their buttocks uppermost. Trousers patched with little patches, doodling threads. Old man erects a stall with a canopy painted with guinea fowl. Pottery not unlike that of ancient

Egypt—gourds, origins of pots and pottery.

Village—round huts, granaries, sandy streets lined with wattle fences and weeds, all shades of ochre and green. The fact that several thousand people can congregate from the hinterland and market. Piles of batteries and soapcakes, tins of tomato puree, Nescafé, safety matches, Sloan's Liniment Kills Pain.

The calabash, orange or yellow or dun coloured, is the symbol of fertility of the mother. Upright, globular, it suggests the form of the womb. The Hausa and Peul women with their plaited hair and cicatrized faces ladle milk from spoons made of smaller calabashes. And you gather from the air of condescension they present it with that you are getting the teat of the Great Mother to suck, not the sourish milk of their goats and cows.

Women wrapped in indigo with coral beads. Arms bangled and gleaming with bead and yellow bone bracelets—rings in pierced ears like curtain rings. Next to the milk-sellers was a broken woman, legs spindled and scabbed, her hair matted not tied with plaits like her companions, when she crouched on the ground not covering her sex. Breasts withered into leathery pouches that never nursed a child. A woman broken in pieces. On her head arranged in a pile broken calabashes, all fragmented like her life yet neatly piled in a pyramid on her head.

Tahoua. Returned early with the hope of sleep, but the noise coming from the bar increased in crescendo, increased and increased. Thumping of fists on the table and songs and more songs which increased in volume and incoherence as the whisky increased. Finally at one-thirty I thought a shot of alcohol might assist sleep, put on my trousers and bought a whisky. The *patronne*, her name is Annie, was surrounded by men, six Negroes and two French. One of the French said, '*Vous n'êtes pas la police?*' and I said I was not and he went on singing and banging. Annie in a long tartan skirt, her auburn hair brushed up and lacquered in a pomade, her eyes reduced to bleary slits, more double-chinned than ever, squealed with false pleasure and her gold teeth glittered in her mouth. '*C'est pour moi, ce chanson.* Zey are zinging zis zong for me. *Ecoute, mon cher,*' and she held me by the ribs and said she was sorry they'd woken me.

Quand on vient à Tahoua
Viens
Voir Annie
Et son whisky
Annie et
Son whisky

—repeated and repeated.

Next morning there was a solemn-faced gentleman with a briefcase, and from the looks of Annie's companion who raised her eyebrows that were hardly raisable any more I guessed the gentleman was the law.

10 January. Lay sweating in the sleeping-bag with the hot/cold sweat around my balls, dodging, waiting for the mosquitoes that lunged around. Cockroach in the room. Husband of Annie left her. Now she hates all white people. She likes Negroes. Only Negroes. White Annie getting laid by the groom. Good for old Annie.

Waited by the same bedraggled tree and waited and they said the truck would come and it didn't. The negro boy with jeans and plastic sandals said it would come, *Je crois, Je crois, Je crois,* he said, but it didn't come because it had gone long ago, or wasn't going to go. Sat by the fenced compound planted with pink oleanders that lay right by the barracks, that might have been a barracks but was a school. Reminded me of Afghanistan with the round silver grey leaves all covered with dust, plants poisonous with mauve and white flowers that were more like boils or pustules than flowers and their fruit green like sagging squashy testicles.

Speckled shade, grass that crackled underfoot, flowers that defy the heat, shrivelled patches of oil. *Mus, mus, mus*—tiny grey kitten howling viciously in a pile of rocks.

Beautiful Hausas in water-blue on black horses, their black faces reflecting the blue of their clothes and the blue of the sky so that they turned the colour of a night sky without a hint of brown in it.

13 January. Half past six. Half past six in the market—one empty lorry, and next to it a couple of Hausas with a smattering of English. Donkey grazing by and a cold, cold wind as the sky turns from indigo to grey. The sound of guinea fowl and cockerels and the thumping of mortars. Light by the petrol pump and the muffled intonation of morning prayer. Morning flight of the vultures till they come to rest on the office of the Compagnie Africaine Française. Figures come out of the shadows, a boy in an orange cap and another veiled and turbanned man, and the lorry begins to fill as if of its own accord.

Pathological wandering has its place among the Peuls. In one of the great nineteenth-century droughts the herdsmen went mad and wandered about the bush chasing phantom cattle.

Kites casting their shadows on the courtyard. A military installation of the French saluted by an old man with colonel's moustache and his head covered by a dishcloth.

They say the Touareg boys are always the most intelligent in the first two years of school, but the novelty of learning rapidly wears off and, conscious of their racial inferiority, they refuse to work. This refusal is of course tantamount to racial suicide. They are gradually being squeezed out and out and further out.

The Bouzous are blackened up Touaregs who live in villages, grow things but speak Tamashek and wear the veil. Rather disquieting.

Peuls are virtually useless when it comes to crafts of any kind. Hausas are energetic businessmen.

Very comfortably installed in the corner of the lorry. Less cold now.

16 January. Will not hire another truck in a hurry. Less uncomfortable last night on the mattress, but a pin stuck into my behind when I moved into one position. Arrived as dawn was breaking and could see the amazing outline of the mosque's minaret, bristling with wooden spires like the vertebra of some defunct fauna. Agadès in the morning light. Another world, the world of the desert. Golden sun hitting the ragged red mud walls, magpies around the mosque and the awful blue of the sky.

The desert men at once recognizable for their white toothy smiles.

The Hausa wrestling match—drugged, gleaming boys, incredibly tough and lean, flexing muscles in animal skins with eyes in the buttocks and tail for nose.

A Hausa house—mud-coloured and on the outside the texture of a good-natured bath towel. Inside, a pillar supporting a vault of thornbush logs. Gummy smell. Door made from the gate of a crate of canned pineapples from the Côte d'Ivoire. Stepped on an old champagne bottle. And a plate that could have been made by a maiden of the Neolithic age. And an old French military camp-bed recovered lovingly with camel leather. It is home. I am happy with it.

Shopping with El Hadj Dilalé. Made to carry everything— sacks, couscous, dirty rice, pinkish rock salt, dried tomatoes, sugar, green tea, etc. Rice from a merchant—'You will find everything else there.' One merchant, very sophisticated and superior with gold teeth and a pink *boubou*, made out measures of couscous in plastic bags. The other a sweet man who kept trying not to ask me too much. Corrected my *boubou* by announcing it was a Bouzou style and therefore inferior.

The trots. Shat in my underpants in the sleeping-bag. Horrible dawn. Decided not to go.

En marche (have lost all track of date). Crested larks and flocks of black parakeets whisking around as they part in flight. Silence but for creaking of the saddles. Camel docile and amenable. Sound of women's laughter like water bubbling from a spring.

The camel has the most elegant arsehole of any beast I know, none of the flushing flesh pink of the rectum which shows in a horse. And it produces the most exquisite turd—a neat elliptical shape which rapidly hardens in the sun. The shape and texture of a pecan nut.

Tahoua, 30 January. Mme Annie held her *soirée musicale* during the night and looked rather the worse for wear this morning.

'Equipe Zaza-Bam-Bam et les Supremes Togolaises.' The Togolese band was of excessive black elegance with expensive electronic equipment in plastic cases that had been patterned in tortoiseshell. The noise of the electric guitars was frightful, full of rhythm but without basic musical taste.

Mme Annie sang:

Si j'étais une cigarette
Entre tes doigts tu me tiendras
Et sous le feu d'une allumette
Je me consumeras pour toi.

The schoolmaster said that the life of the Peuls was unique. That the death of a cow which had borne six calves was of infinitely more account than the death of a parent—a cause for wailing and mournful vigils. In order to get the children to school they (the authorities) have to beseech a chief (resident in Tahoua) for his active participation. Otherwise they disappear into the bush—to Mali or Tchad—and are never heard of again.

Visited a local village stretched out on the flank of a hill with one solitary white house. Then returned to town to watch the break up of a political meeting at the Maison du Parti. A single-roomed mud structure just below the abattoir where the morning's subject was the sexual freedom of teenagers.

Birnin N'konni, 5 February. Have been in Africa for a month only and it seems an age. Nothing particular to record except the extraordinary silhouette in profile of the Vietnamienne. How I wish I could penetrate her thoughts. She has a slight cold this morning. The dust-coloured poodle still ever present.

Slept in the Martiniquais's house in a proper bed this time, not on the floor. He complained that the alphabetization programme is synonymous with the learning of French. No suggestion that Hausa or Djima or Tamashek might even be put into letters. The effect is supposed to make the whole nation speak French and intensify its ties to France. I wonder. I believe the French speakers develop a sense of frustration, inadequacy and loathing for France. The President maintained the view—not an unacceptable view—that it was better to be neocolonialized by people one had partly got rid of than to let down the floodgates to unknown ideologies tinged with oriental fanaticism.

Le Lotus Bleu. Small Vietnamese crêpes submerged in a sauce to which one adds another sauce which cancels out the taste of the first sauce. The crêpe is then ready to be enfolded in a lettuce leaf and a sprig of fresh mint. The taste of the fresh mint cancels out the taste of the second sauce.

Houses like aquariums. Concrete walls. Baby-blue gates. Children playing roundy-roundy in a blue and white mosaic podium like an inverted swimming-pool.

The bus. God, what have I let myself in for? I am the last passenger, the ultimate miracle in overstuffing an African bus. First Class in the train after this. To Abomey. To the place charmingly called Dassa Zoumé.

A lady with her hair tied up in three-inch spikes like classical personifications of the dawn, the illusion intensified by the cloud of dawn-pink gauze wrapped about it. Her baby's mouth never leaves her breast, its hand never leaves her mouth.

Dahomey. This country—about which I know absolutely nothing— will forever remain fixed in my mind as the land of the decent train. I was—as I said—the ultimate passenger in the overstuffed bus and only succeeded in browbeating my way into it by sheer force of personality—that is, white bloodymindedness. The last passenger at the edge of the town was an enormous Negress in blue and white print who heaved herself in as well. Feeling remorse for my behaviour I let her pass—as a lady—a thing no African would dream of doing. This was a bad thing. She monopolized my precious extra three inches of leg room. Worse, she brought two infant children. One she treated as a headscarf, the other as a handbag. She also had a large enamel basin full of millet balls, chicken, pineapple, papaya and hard-boiled eggs—none of which she shared out to anyone. I was forced to sit on the edge—hard edge—of a tin trunk in between a dreamy long individual's legs. The journey lasted fourteen hours. Arrived in Parakou to the hotel where the staff of the Routier's I shall always remember with gratitude. May even send them a postcard. They provided *café-au-lait*, butter, *confiture fraise*, hot fresh bread in two minutes flat. Then got me a taxi and on to the train with two minutes to spare.

233

Abomey. Vegetation. Total change. It will take me some time to get used to it. Depressing effects of slack and lava. Dead black skeletons. Big black phallus-like pods in the trees which have no flower. Same family as jacaranda and acacia.

If we have moved into a new vegetational world, we have certainly moved into a new gastronomic one. Consider lunch. Aperitif—coconut milk. Followed by grilled agouti, yams, pineapple. The meat of the agouti was rich and gamey and not a bit tough. The locals hunt it with bows and arrows.

The palace of the Kings of Dahomey. Architecturally unimportant but not at all displeasing. Long low thatched halls with polychromed plaques—now of course refurbished—which served to instruct the kings in their own history and prowess. The series of thrones, dating back to 1600, perfectly preserved, was particularly interesting—also the ceremonial standards of beaten bronze which didn't change in style over three hundred years. Cutlery presented by English in return for trade concessions.

Cotonou, 9 February. Have made a bad start with the Hotel de Port, imagining some sort of old-style joint where the poor whites congregate for a Ricard and whore. Instead the most elaborate motel with *piscine* and thatched beach cottages. The outside looked not unpromising but concealed the deadly Tropical-Americanization of the interior. It is rather pathetic the degree to which the ex-colons will go to preserve their gastronomic links with France. I am eating a *Bresse Bleu* which has blushed a sort of apricot pink in the tropics.

Hard still to take it in. The sheds of corrugated iron, armadillo-ish in appearance, rusting and covered with a rust-coloured dust. The stations where the women sell custard apples. The smells. Sweat, fruit, dust. The stunted goats. On the beach the straight line of white breakers, a pale blue sea, the colour almost of the sky. The bleached hulls of the pirogues. The blown coconut palms.

Leaving Cotonou for Ouidah with high rain clouds building up, perhaps for a storm.

PAUL AUSTER
THE RED NOTEBOOK

In 1973 I was offered a job as caretaker of a farmhouse in the south of France. My on-again off-again romance with a young woman named L. seemed to be on again, so we decided to join forces and take the job together. We had both run out of money by then, and without this offer we would have been compelled to return to America—which neither of us wanted to do just yet.

The place was beautiful: a large, eighteenth-century stone house bordered by vineyards on one side and a national forest on the other. The nearest village was two kilometres away, but it was inhabited by no more than forty people, none of whom was under sixty or seventy years old. It was an ideal spot for two young writers to spend a year, and L. and I both worked hard there, accomplishing more in that house than either one of us would have thought possible.

But we lived permanently on the brink of catastrophe. Our employers, an American couple who lived in Paris, sent us a small monthly salary (fifty dollars), a gas allowance for the car and money to feed the two Labrador retrievers who were part of the household. All in all, it was a generous arrangement. There was no rent to pay, and even if our salary fell short of what we needed to live on, it gave us a head start on each month's expenses. Our plan was to earn the rest by doing translations. Before leaving Paris and settling in the country, we had set up a number of jobs to see us through the year. What we had neglected to take into account was that publishers are often slow to pay their bills. We had also forgotten to consider that cheques sent from one country to another can take weeks to clear, and that once they do, bank charges and exchange fees cut into the amounts. Since L. and I had left no margin for error, we often found ourselves in quite desperate straits.

I remember savage nicotine fits, my body numb with need as I scrounged among sofa cushions and crawled behind cupboards in search of loose coins. For eighteen centimes (about three and a half cents), you could buy a brand of cigarettes called Parisiennes, which were sold in packs of four. I remember feeding the dogs and thinking that they ate better than I did. I remember conversations with L. when we seriously considered opening a can of dog food and eating it for dinner.

Our only other source of income came from a man named

James Sugar (I don't mean to insist on metaphorical names, but facts are facts, and there's nothing I can do about it.) Sugar worked as a staff photographer for *National Geographic* and was collaborating with one of our employers on an article about the region. He took pictures for several months, criss-crossing Provence in a rented car provided by his magazine, and whenever he was nearby he would spend the night with us. Since the magazine also provided him with an expense account, he would very graciously slip us the money that had been allotted for his hotel costs. If I remember correctly, the sum came to fifty francs a night. In effect, L. and I became his private innkeepers, and as Sugar was an amiable man, we were always glad to see him. The only problem was that we never knew when he was going to turn up. He never called in advance, and weeks could go by between his visits. We therefore learned not to count on Mr Sugar. He would arrive out of nowhere, pulling up in front of the house in his shiny blue car, stay for a night or two, and then disappear again. Each time he left, we assumed that was the last time we would ever see him.

The worst moments came for us in the late winter and early spring. Cheques failed to arrive, one of the dogs was stolen and little by little we ate our way through the stockpile of food in the kitchen. In the end, we had nothing left but a bag of onions, a bottle of cooking oil and a packaged pie-crust that someone had bought before we moved into the house—a remnant from the previous summer. L. and I held out all morning and into the afternoon, but by two-thirty hunger had got the better of us, and so we went into the kitchen to prepare our last meal. Given the paucity of ingredients, an onion pie was the only dish that made sense.

After our concoction had been in the oven for what seemed a sufficient length of time, we took it out, set it on the table and dug in. Against all our expectations, we both found it delicious. I think we even went so far as to say that it was the best food we had ever tasted, but no doubt that was a feeble attempt to keep our spirits up. Once we had chewed a little more, however, disappointment set in. Reluctantly—ever so reluctantly—we were forced to admit that the pie had not yet cooked through, that the centre was still too cold to eat. There was nothing to be done but put it back in the oven for another ten or fifteen minutes. Considering our hunger,

237

and considering that our salivary glands had just been activated, relinquishing the pie was not easy.

To stifle our impatience, we went outside for a brief stroll, thinking the time would pass more quickly if we removed ourselves from the good smells in the kitchen. As I remember it, we circled the house once, perhaps twice. Perhaps we drifted into a deep conversation about something (I can't remember), but however it happened, and however long we were gone, by the time we entered the house again the kitchen was filled with smoke. We rushed to the oven and pulled out the pie, but it was too late. Our meal was dead. It had been incinerated, burned to a charred and blackened mass, and not one morsel could be salvaged.

It sounds like a funny story now, but at the time it was anything but funny. We had fallen into a dark hole, and neither one of us could think of a way to get out. In all my years of struggling to be a man, I doubt there has ever been a moment when I felt less inclined to laugh or crack jokes. This was really the end, and it was a terrible and frightening place to be.

That was at four o'clock in the afternoon. Less than an hour later, the errant Mr Sugar suddenly appeared, driving up to the house in a cloud of dust, gravel and dirt crunching all around him. If I think about it hard enough, I can still see his naïve and goofy smile as he bounced out of the car and said hello. It was a miracle. It was a genuine miracle, and I was there to witness it with my own eyes. Until that moment, I had thought those things happened only in books.

Sugar treated us to dinner that night in a two-star restaurant. We ate copiously and well, we emptied several bottles of wine, we laughed our heads off. And yet, delicious as that food must have been, I can't remember a thing about it. But I have never forgotten the taste of the onion pie.

2

Not long after I returned to New York (July, 1974), a friend told me the following story. It is set in Yugoslavia, during what must have been the last months of the Second World War.

S.'s uncle was a member of a Serbian partisan group that fought against the Nazi occupation. One morning, he and his comrades woke up to find themselves surrounded by German troops. They were holed up in a farmhouse somewhere in the country, a foot of snow lay on the ground and there was no escape. Not knowing what else to do, the men decided to draw lots. Their plan was to burst out of the farmhouse one by one, dash through the snow and see if they couldn't make it to safety. S.'s uncle was supposed to go third.

He watched through the window as the first man ran out into the snow-covered field. There was a barrage of machine-gun fire from the woods, and the man was cut down. A moment later, the second man ran out, and the same thing happened. The machine-guns blasted, and he fell down dead in the snow.

Then it was my friend's uncle's turn. I don't know if he hesitated at the doorway; I don't know what thoughts were pounding through his head at that moment. The only thing I was told was that he started to run, charging through the snow for all he was worth. It seemed as if he ran forever. Then, suddenly, he felt pain in his leg. A second after that, an overpowering warmth spread through his body, and a second after that he lost consciousness.

When he woke up, he found himself lying on his back in a peasant's cart. He had no idea how much time had elapsed or how he had been rescued. He had simply opened his eyes—and there he was, lying in a cart that some horse or mule was pulling down a country road, staring up at the back of a peasant's head. He studied the back of that head for several seconds, and then loud explosions erupted from the woods. Too weak to move, he kept looking at the back of the head, and suddenly it was gone. It just flew off the peasant's body, and where a moment before there had been a whole man, there was now a man without a head.

More noise, more confusion. Whether the horse went on pulling the cart or not I can't say, but within minutes, perhaps even seconds, a large contingent of Russian troops came rolling down the road. Jeeps, tanks, scores of soldiers. When the commanding officer took a look at S.'s uncle's leg, he quickly dispatched him to an infirmary that had been set up in the neighbourhood. It was no more than a rickety wooden shack—a hen-house, maybe, or an outbuilding on some farm. There the Russian army doctor pronounced the leg past saving. It was too severely damaged, he said, and he was going to have to cut it off.

My friend's uncle began to scream. 'Don't cut off my leg,' he cried. 'Please, I beg of you, don't cut off my leg!' But no one listened to him. The medics strapped him to the operating table, and the doctor picked up his saw. Just as he was about to pierce the skin of the leg, there was another explosion. The roof of the infirmary collapsed, the walls fell down, the entire place was obliterated. And once again, S.'s uncle lost consciousness.

When he woke up this time, he found himself lying in a bed. The sheets were clean and soft, there were pleasant smells in the room and his leg was still attached to his body. A moment later, he was looking into the face of a beautiful young woman. She was smiling at him and feeding him broth with a spoon. It seemed possible to him that he had woken up in heaven. With no knowledge of how it had happened, he had been rescued again and carried to another farmhouse.

He stayed on in the house and fell in love with the beautiful young woman, but nothing ever came of the romance. I wish I could say why, but S. never filled me in on the details. I know only that his uncle kept his leg, and that once the war was over, he moved to America to begin a new life. Somehow or other (the circumstances are obscure to me), he wound up as an insurance salesman in Chicago.

3

L. and I were married in 1974. Our son Daniel was born in 1977, but by the following year our marriage had ended. None of that is relevant now—except to set the scene for an incident that took place in the spring of 1980.

We were both living in Brooklyn then, about three or four blocks from each other, and our son divided his time between the two apartments. One morning, I had to stop by L.'s place to pick up Daniel and walk him to nursery school. Just as we were about to walk off together, L. opened the window of her third-floor apartment to throw me some money. Perhaps she wanted me to replenish a parking meter for her or do an errand, I don't know. All that remains is the open window and the image of a dime flying through the air. I see it with such clarity; it's almost as if I have studied photographs of that instant, as if it's part of a recurring dream I've had ever since.

But the dime hit the branch of a tree, and its downward arc into my hand was disrupted. It bounced off the tree, landed soundlessly somewhere nearby and then it was gone. I remember bending down and searching the pavement, digging among the leaves and twigs at the base of the tree, but the dime was nowhere to be found.

I can place that event in early spring because later the same day I attended a baseball game at Shea Stadium—the opening game of the season. A friend of mine had been offered tickets, and he had generously invited me to go along with him. I had never been to an opening game before, and I remember the occasion well.

We arrived early (something about collecting the tickets at a certain window), and as my friend went off to complete the transaction, I waited for him outside one of the entrances to the stadium. Not a single soul was around. I ducked into a little alcove to light a cigarette (a strong wind was blowing that day), and there, sitting on the ground not two inches from my feet, was a dime. I bent down, picked it up and put it in my pocket. Ridiculous as it might sound, I felt certain that it was the same dime I had lost in Brooklyn that morning.

4

In my son's nursery school, there was a little girl whose parents were going through a divorce. I particularly liked her father, a struggling painter who earned his living by doing architectural renderings. His paintings were quite beautiful, I thought, but he never had much luck in convincing dealers to support his work. The one time he did have a show, the gallery promptly went out of business.

B. was not an intimate friend, but we enjoyed each other's

company, and whenever I saw him I would return home with renewed admiration for his steadfastness and inner calm. He was not a man who grumbled or felt sorry for himself. However gloomy things had become for him in recent years (endless money problems, lack of artistic success, threats of eviction from his landlord, difficulties with his ex-wife), none of it seemed to throw him off course. He continued to paint with the same passion as ever, and unlike so many others, he never expressed any bitterness or envy towards less talented artists who were doing better than he was.

When he wasn't working on his own canvasses, he would sometimes go to the Metropolitan Museum and make copies of the old masters. I remember a Caravaggio he once did that struck me as utterly remarkable. It wasn't a copy so much as a replica, an exact duplication of the original. On one of those visits to the museum, a Texas millionaire spotted B. at work and was so impressed that he commissioned him to do a copy of a Renoir painting—which he then presented to his fiancée as a gift.

B. was exceedingly tall (six-five or six-six), good-looking and gentle in his manner—qualities that made him especially attractive to women. Once his divorce was behind him and he began to circulate again, he had no trouble finding female companions. I saw him only about two or three times a year, and each time there was another woman in his life. All of them were obviously mad for him, but for one reason or another, none of these affairs lasted very long.

After two or three years, B.'s landlord finally made good on his threats and evicted him from his loft. B. moved out of the city, and I lost touch with him.

Several more years went by, and then one night B. came back to town to attend a dinner party. My wife and I were also there, and since we knew that B. was about to get married, we asked him to tell us the story of how he had met his future wife.

About six months earlier, he said, he had been talking to a friend on the phone. This friend was worried about him, and after a while he began to scold B. for not having married again. You've been divorced for seven years now, he said, and in that time you could have settled down with any one of a dozen attractive and remarkable women. But no one is ever good enough for you, and you've turned them all away. What's wrong with you, B.? What in the world do you want?

There's nothing wrong with me, B. said. I just haven't found the right person, that's all.

At the rate you're going, you never will, the friend answered. I mean, have you ever met one woman who comes close to what you're looking for? Name one. I dare you to name just one.

Startled by his friend's vehemence, B. paused to consider the question carefully. Yes, he finally said, there was one. A woman by the name of E., whom he had known as a student at Harvard more than twenty years ago. But she had been involved with another man at the time, and he had been involved with another woman (his future ex-wife), and nothing had developed between them. He had no idea where E. was now, he said, but if he could meet someone like her, he knew he wouldn't hesitate to get married again.

That was the end of the conversation. Until mentioning her to his friend, B. hadn't thought about this woman in over ten years, but now that she had resurfaced in his mind, he had trouble thinking about anything else. For the next three or four days, he thought about her constantly, unable to shake the feeling that his one chance for happiness had been lost many years ago. Then, almost as if the intensity of these thoughts had sent a signal out into the world, the phone rang one night, and there was E. on the other end of the line.

B. kept her on the phone for more than three hours. He scarcely knew what he said to her, but he went on talking until past midnight, understanding that something momentous had happened and that he mustn't let her escape again.

After graduating from college, E. had joined a dance company, and for the past twenty years she had devoted herself exclusively to her career. She had never married, and now that she was about to retire as a performer, she was calling old friends from her past, trying to make contact with the world again. She had no family (her parents had been killed in a car crash when she was a small girl) and had been raised by two aunts, both of whom were now dead.

B. arranged to see her the next night. Once they were together, it didn't take long for him to discover that his feelings for her were just as strong as he had imagined. He fell in love with her all over again, and several weeks later they were engaged to be married.

To make the story even more perfect, it turned out that E. was independently wealthy. Her aunts had been rich, and after they died she had inherited all their money—which meant that not only had B. found true love, but the crushing money problems that had plagued him for so many years had suddenly vanished. All in one fell swoop.

A year or two after the wedding, they had a child. At last report, mother, father and baby were doing just fine.

5

Twelve years ago, my wife's sister went off to live in Taiwan. Her intention was to study Chinese (which she now speaks with breathtaking fluency) and to support herself by giving English lessons to native Chinese speakers in Taipei. That was approximately one year before I met my wife, who was then a graduate student at Columbia University.

One day, my future sister-in-law was talking to an American friend, a young woman who had also gone to Taipei to study Chinese. The conversation came around to the subject of their families back home, which in turn led to the following exchange:

'I have a sister who lives in New York,' my future sister-in-law said.

'So do I,' her friend answered.

'My sister lives on the Upper West Side.'

'So does mine.'

'My sister lives on West 109th Street.'

'Believe it or not, so does mine.'

'My sister lives at 309 West 109th Street.'

'So does mine!'

'My sister lives on the second floor of 309 West 109th Street.'

The friend took a deep breath and said, 'I know this sounds crazy, but so does mine.'

It is scarcely possible for two cities to be farther apart than Taipei and New York. They are at opposite ends of the earth, separated by a distance of more than ten thousand miles, and when it is day in one it is night in the other. As the two young women in

Taipei marvelled over the astounding connection they had just uncovered, they realized that their two sisters were probably asleep at that moment. On the same floor of the same building in northern Manhattan, each one was sleeping in her own apartment, unaware of the conversation that was taking place about them on the other side of the world

Although they were neighbours, the two sisters in New York did not know each other. When they finally met (two years later), neither one was living in that building any more.

Siri and I were married then. One evening, on our way to an appointment somewhere, we happened to stop in at a bookstore on Broadway to browse for a few minutes. We must have wandered into different aisles, and because Siri wanted to show me something, or because I wanted to show her something (I can't remember), one of us spoke the other's name out loud. A second later, a woman came rushing up to us. 'You're Paul Auster and Siri Hustvedt, aren't you?' she said. 'Yes,' we said, 'that's exactly who we are. How did you know that?' The woman then explained that her sister and Siri's sister had been students together in Taiwan.

The circle had been closed at last. Since that evening in the bookstore ten years ago, this woman has been one of our best and most loyal friends.

6

C. is a French poet. We have known each other for more than twenty years now, and while we don't see each other often (he lives in Paris and I live in New York), the bond between us remains strong. It is a fraternal bond, somehow, as if in some former life we had actually been brothers.

C. is a man of manifold contradictions. He is both open to the world and shut off from it, a charismatic figure with scores of friends everywhere (legendary for his kindness, his humour, his conversation) and yet someone who has been wounded by life, who struggles to perform the simple tasks that most other people take for granted. An exceptionally gifted poet and thinker about poetry, C. is nevertheless hampered by frequent writing blocks, streaks of morbid self-doubt and surprisingly (for someone so generous), a capacity for long-standing grudges and quarrels, usually over some trifle or abstract principle. No one is more universally admired than C.; no one has more talent; no one so readily commands attention; and yet he has always done everything in his power to marginalize himself. Since his separation from his wife many years ago, he has lived alone in a number of small, one-room apartments, subsisting on almost no money and only fitful bouts of employment, publishing little and refusing to write a single word of criticism, even though he reads everything and knows more about contemporary poetry than anyone else in France. To those of us who love him (and we are many), C. is often a cause of concern. To the degree that we respect him and care about his well-being, we also worry about him.

He had a rough childhood. I can't say to what extent that explains anything, but the facts should not be overlooked. His father apparently ran off with another woman when C. was a little boy, and after that my friend grew up an only child with no family life to speak of, alone with his mother. I have never met C.'s mother, but by all accounts she is a bizarre character. She went through a series of love affairs during C.'s childhood and adolescence, each with a man younger than the man before him. By the time C. left home to enter the army at the age of twenty-one, his mother's boyfriend was scarcely older than he was. In more recent years, the central purpose of her life has been a campaign to promote the canonization of a certain Italian priest (whose name eludes me now). She has besieged the Catholic authorities with countless letters extolling the holiness of this man, and at one point she even commissioned an artist to create a life-size statue of him— which now stands in her front yard as an enduring testament to her cause.

Although not a father himself, C. became a kind of pseudo-father seven or eight years ago. After a falling out with his girl-friend (during which they temporarily broke up), she had a brief affair with another man and became pregnant. The affair ended almost at once, but she decided to have the baby on her own. A little girl was born, and even though C. is not her real father, he has devoted himself to her since the day of her birth and adores her as if she were his own flesh and blood.

One day about four years ago, C. happened to be visiting a friend. In the apartment there was a *Minitel*, a small computer given out for free by the French telephone company. Among other things, the *Minitel* contains the address and phone number of every person in France. As C. sat there playing with his friend's new machine, it suddenly occurred to him to look up his father's address. He found it in Lyon. When he returned home later that day, he stuffed one of his books into an envelope and sent it off to the address in Lyon—initiating the first contact with his father in over forty years. Until he found himself doing these things, it had never even crossed his mind that he wanted to do them.

That same night, he ran into another friend in a café—a woman psychoanalyst—and told her about these strange, unpremeditated acts. It was as if he had felt his father calling out to him, he said, as if some uncanny force had unleashed itself inside him. Considering that he had absolutely no memories of the man, he couldn't even begin to guess when they had last seen each other.

The woman thought for a moment and said, 'How old is L.?', referring to C.'s girlfriend's daughter.

'Three and a half,' C. answered.

'I can't be sure,' the woman said, 'but I'd be willing to bet that you were three and a half the last time you saw your father. I say that because you love L. so much. Your identification with her is very strong and you're reliving your life through her.'

Several days after that, there was a reply from Lyon—a warm and perfectly gracious letter from C.'s father. After thanking C. for the book, he went on to tell him how proud he was to learn that his son had grown up to become a writer. By pure coincidence, he added, the package had been mailed on his birthday, and he was very moved by the symbolism of the gesture.

None of this tallied with the stories C. had heard throughout his childhood. According to his mother, his father was a monster of selfishness who had walked out on her for a 'slut' and had never wanted anything to do with his son. C. had believed these stories and had shied away from any contact with his father. Now, on the strength of this letter, he no longer knew what to believe.

He decided to write back. The tone of his response was

guarded, but nevertheless it was a response. Within days he received another reply, and this second letter was just as warm and gracious as the first had been. C. and his father began a correspondence. It went on for a month or two, and eventually C. began to consider travelling down to Lyon to meet his father face to face.

Before he could make any definite plans, he received a letter from his father's wife informing him that his father was dead. He had been in ill health for the past several years, she wrote, but the recent exchange of letters with C. had given him great happiness, and his last days had been filled with optimism and joy.

It was at this moment that I first heard about the incredible reversals that had taken place in C.'s life. Sitting on the train from Paris to Lyon (on his way to visit his 'stepmother' for the first time), he wrote me a letter that sketched out the story of the past month. His handwriting registered each jolt of the tracks, as if the speed of the train were an exact image of the thoughts racing through his head. As he put it somewhere in that letter: 'I feel as if I've become a character in one of your novels.'

His father's wife could not have been friendlier to him during the visit. Among other things, C. learned that his father had suffered a heart attack on the morning of his last birthday (the day that C. had looked up his address on the Minitel) and that, yes, C. had been precisely three and a half years old at the time of his parents' divorce. His stepmother then went on to tell him the story of his life from his father's point of view—which contradicted everything his mother had ever told him. In this version, it was his mother who had walked out on his father; it was his mother who had forbidden his father from seeing him; it was his mother who had broken his father's heart. She told C. how his father would come around to the schoolyard when C. was a little boy to look at him through the fence. C. remembered that man, but, not knowing who he was, had been afraid.

C.'s life had now become two lives. There was Version A and Version B, and both were his story. He had lived them both in equal measure, two truths that cancelled each other out, and all along, without even knowing it, he had been stranded in the middle.

His father had owned a small stationery store (the usual stock of paper and writing materials, along with a rental library of popular books). The business had earned him a living, but not much more, and the estate he left behind was quite modest. The numbers are unimportant, however. What counts is that C.'s stepmother (by then an old woman) insisted on splitting the money with him half and half. There was nothing in the will that required her to do that, and morally speaking she needn't have parted with a single penny of her husband's savings. She did it because she wanted to, because it made her happier to share the money than to keep it for herself.

7

In thinking about friendship, particularly about how some friendships endure and others don't, I am reminded of the fact that in all my years of driving I have had just four flat tyres, and that on each occasion the same person was in the car with me (in three different countries, spread out over a period of eight or nine years). J. was a college friend, and though there was always an edge of unease and conflict in our relations, for a time we were close. One spring, while we were still undergraduates, we borrowed my father's ancient station-wagon and drove up into the wilderness of Quebec. The seasons change more slowly in that part of the world, and winter was not yet over. The first flat tyre did not present a problem (we were equipped with a spare), but when a second tyre blew out less than an hour later, we were stranded in the bleak and frigid countryside for most of the day. At the time, I shrugged off the incident as a piece of bad luck, but four or five years later, when J. came to France to visit the house where L. and I were working as caretakers, the same thing happened. We went to Aix-en-Provence for the day (a drive of about two hours) and coming back late that night on a dark, back-country road, we had another flat. Just a coincidence, I thought, and then pushed the event out of my mind. But then, four years after that, in the waning months of my marriage to L., J. came to visit us again—this time in New York state, where L. and I were living with the infant Daniel. At one point, J. and I climbed into the car to go to the store and shop for dinner. I pulled the car out of the garage, turned it around in the rutted dirt driveway and advanced to the edge of the road. Just then, as I waited for a car to pass by, I heard the unmistakable hiss of escaping air. Another tyre had gone flat, and this time we hadn't even left the house. J. and I both laughed, of course, but the truth is that our friendship never really recovered from that fourth flat tyre. I'm not saying that the flat tyres were responsible for our drifting apart, but in some perverse way they were an emblem of how things had always stood between us. I don't want to exaggerate, but even now I can't quite bring myself to reject those flat tyres as meaningless. For the fact is that J. and I have lost contact, and we have not spoken to each other in more than ten years.

8

One afternoon many years ago, my father's car stalled at a red light. A terrible storm was raging, and at the exact moment his engine went dead, lightning struck a large tree by the side of the road. The trunk of the tree split in two, and as my father struggled to get the car started again (unaware that the upper half of the tree was about to fall), the driver of the car behind him, seeing what was about to happen, put his foot on the accelerator and pushed my father's car through the intersection. An instant later, the tree came crashing to the ground, landing in the very spot where my father's car had just been. What was very nearly the end of him proved to be no more than a close call, a brief episode in the ongoing story of his life.

A year or two after that, my father was working on the roof of a building in Jersey City. Somehow or other (I wasn't there to witness it), he slipped off the edge and started falling to the ground. Once again he was headed for certain disaster, and once again he was saved. A clothesline broke his fall, and he walked away from the accident with only a few bumps and bruises. Not even concussion. Not a single broken bone.

That same year, our neighbours across the street hired two men to paint their house. One worker fell off the roof and was killed.

The little girl who lived in that house happened to be my sister's best friend. One winter night, the two of them went to a costume party (they were six or seven years old, and I was nine or ten). It had been arranged that my father would pick them up after the party, and I went along to keep him company. It was bitter cold, and the roads were covered with treacherous sheets of ice. My father drove carefully, and we made the journey back and forth without incident. As we pulled up in front of the little girl's house, however, a number of unlikely events occurred all at once.

My sister's friend was dressed as a fairy princess. To complete the outfit, she had borrowed a pair of her mother's high heels, and every step she took was turned into an adventure. My father stopped the car and climbed out to accompany her to the front door. I was in the back with the girls and had to get out first. I remember standing on the kerb as my sister's friend disentangled herself from the seat, and just as she stepped into the open air, I noticed that the car was rolling slowly in reverse—either because of the ice or because my father had forgotten to engage the emergency brake (I don't know)—but before I could tell my father what was happening, my sister's friend touched the kerb with her mother's high heels and slipped. She went skidding under the car—which was still moving—and there she was, about to be crushed to death by the wheels of my father's Chevy. As I remember it, she didn't make a sound. Without pausing to think, I bent down from the kerb, grabbed hold of her right hand and in one quick gesture yanked her to the sidewalk. An instant later, my father finally noticed that the car was moving. He jumped back into the driver's seat, stepped on the brake and brought the machine to a halt. From start to finish, the whole chain of misadventures couldn't have taken more than eight or ten seconds.

For years afterwards, I walked around feeling that this had been my finest moment. I had actually saved someone's life, and in retrospect I was always astonished by how quickly I had acted, by how sure my movements had been at the critical juncture. Again and again I relived the sensation of pulling that little girl out from under the car.

About two years after that night, our family moved to another house. My sister lost touch with her friend, and I myself did not see her for another fifteen years.

It was June, and my sister and I had both come back to town for a short visit. Just by chance, her old friend dropped by to say hello. She was all grown up now, a young woman of twenty-two who had graduated from college earlier that month, and I must say that I felt some pride in seeing that she had made it to adulthood in one piece. In a casual sort of way, I mentioned the night I had pulled her out from under the car. I was curious to know how well she remembered her brush with death, but from the look on her face, it was clear that she remembered nothing. A blank stare. A slight frown. A shrug. She remembered nothing!

I realized then that she hadn't known the car was moving. She hadn't even known that she was in danger. The whole incident had taken place in a flash: ten seconds of her life, an interval of no account, and none of it had left the slightest mark on her. For me, those seconds had been a defining experience.

Most of all, it stuns me to acknowledge that I am talking about something that happened in 1956 or 1957—and that the little girl of that night is now over forty years old.

9

My first novel was inspired by a wrong number. I was alone in my apartment in Brooklyn one afternoon, sitting at my desk and trying to work, when the telephone rang. If I am not mistaken, it was the spring of 1980, not many days after I found the dime outside Shea Stadium.

I picked up the receiver, and the man on the other end asked if he was talking to the Pinkerton Agency. I told him no, he had dialled the wrong number, and hung up. Then I went back to work and promptly forgot about the call.

The next afternoon, the telephone rang again. It turned out to be the same person asking the same question I had been asked the day before: 'Is this the Pinkerton Agency?' Again I said no, and again I hung up. This time, however, I started thinking about what would have happened if I had said yes. What if I had pretended to be a detective from the Pinkerton Agency? I wondered. What if I had actually taken on the case?

To tell the truth, I felt that I had squandered a rare opportunity. If the man ever called again, I told myself, I would at least talk to him and try to find out what was going on. I waited, but the third call never came.

After that, wheels started turning in my head, and little by little an entire world of possibilities opened up to me. When I sat down to write *City of Glass* a year later, the wrong number had been transformed into the crucial event of the book, the mistake that sets the whole story in motion. A man named Quinn receives a phone call from someone who wants to talk to Paul Auster, the private detective. Just as I did, Quinn tells the caller he has dialled the wrong number. It happens again the next night, and again Quinn hangs up. Unlike me, however, Quinn is given another chance. When the phone rings again on the third night, he plays along with the caller and takes on the case. Yes, he says, I'm Paul Auster—and at that moment the madness begins.

All well and good. I finished the book ten years ago, and since then I have gone on to occupy myself with other projects, other ideas, other books. Less than two months ago, however, I learned that books are never finished, that it is possible for stories to go on writing themselves without an author.

I was alone in my apartment in Brooklyn, sitting at my desk and trying to work, when the telephone rang. This was a different apartment from the one I had in 1980—with a different telephone number. I picked up the receiver, and the man on the other end asked if he could speak to Mr Quinn. He had a Spanish accent and I did not recognize the voice. For a moment I thought it might be one of my friends trying to pull my leg. 'Mr Quinn?' I said. 'Is this some kind of joke or what?'

No, it wasn't a joke. The man was in dead earnest. He had to talk to Mr Quinn, and would I please put him on the line. Just to make sure, I asked him to spell out the name. The caller's accent was quite thick, and I was hoping that he wanted to talk to a Mr Queen. 'Q-U-I-N-N,' the man answered. I suddenly grew scared, and for a moment or two I couldn't get any words out of my mouth. 'I'm sorry,' I said at last, 'there's no Mr Quinn here. You've dialled the wrong number.' The man apologized for disturbing me, and then we both hung up.

This really happened. Like everything else I have set down in this red notebook, it is a true story.

Notes on Contributors

Tracy Kidder has been a regular, if not daily, visitor of the Linda Manor nursing home since not long after it opened in 1990. He is forty-seven and the author of three other books of non-fiction: *The Soul of a New Machine*, *Home* and *Among Schoolchildren*. 'The Last Place on Earth' is taken from *Old Friends*. It is available in the United States from Houghton Mifflin. **Mary Karr** has recently published her second volume of poetry, *The Devil's Tour*. 'Grandma Moore's Cancer', her first published piece of prose, will be included in the memoir that she is now writing, *The Liar's Club*, which Viking in New York will publish in two years. **Charles Glass** is the author of *Tribes with Flags*, about his time in the Lebanon. He is currently in Bosnia, reporting for ABC News. The seven hundred twenty page **Collected Stories of T.Coraghessan Boyle** will be published as a paperback original by Granta Books in October. *The Road to Wellville*, his new novel, about Doctor Kellogg and the origins of health fanaticism, is being filmed by Alan Parker. **Nadine Gordimer** received the Nobel Prize for Literature in 1991. **Maggie O'Kane** was named Journalist of the Year at the British Press Awards for her reporting from the former Yugoslavia for the *Guardian*. Since Christmas, **Thomas Kern** has spent less than one week outside the former Yugoslavia. **Amitav Ghosh** is the author of two novels, *The Circle of Reason* and *The Shadow Lines*, and the recently published *In an Antique Land*, a highly personal account—part travel book, part history—of life in an Egyptian village. **Tobias Wolff** is completing a novel inspired by his time in Vietnam. **Ivan Klíma**'s most recent novel, *My Golden Trades*, won the *Independent*'s Foreign Fiction Award. It has just been published in paperback. **Paul Theroux**'s novella 'Lady Max' appeared in *Granta* 40. Both **Bruce Chatwin**'s photographs and his notebooks will be published for the first time in one volume in October—by Jonathan Cape in Britain and Viking in the United States. **Paul Auster** is the author of *The New York Trilogy*. The complete 'Red Notebook' will be included in a collection of essays, prefaces and interviews, *The Art of Hunger*, published this autumn.

Note: The full version of Pawel Huelle's story, 'The Table', published in *Granta* 42, will be included in *Moving House*, to be published by Bloomsbury next year. Christa Wolf's 'Liberation Day,' published in the same issue, is included in her new collection, *What Remains and Other Stories*, available in Britain from Virago Books and in the United States from Farrar, Straus & Giroux.